THE TOP

Chelsea

IT'S NOT TRIVIA, IT'S MORE IMPORTANT THAN THAT

ROUGH GUIDE
11s

Written by
Tim Harrison

Text editors
Paul Simpson, Helen Rodiss,
Michaela Bushell

Production
Ian Cranna, Tim Oldham, Tim
Harrison, Ann Oliver

Cover and book design
Sharon O'Connor

Cover image
Age Fotostock/Superstock

Thanks to
Rick Glanvill, Cliff Port,
Dave Sells, Paul Lagan,
Alan Golden, Peter Crutchfield,
Alan Humphrey, Mark
Ellingham, Andrew Lockett,
Simon Kanter... and Jane, who
has now got the dining room
table back

**Printed in Spain
by Graphy Cems**

This edition published
July 2005 was prepared by
Haymarket Network for
Rough Guides Ltd,
80 Strand, London, WC2R ORL

Distributed by Penguin Group
Penguin Books Ltd,
27 Wrights Lane,
London W8 5TZ

A catalogue record for this
book is available from the
British Library.
ISBN 1-84353-562-9

Contents

ABSOLUTE BEST MOMENTS

11 days of blue heaven

1. The climax of the 2004/05 season

Chelsea's first title in 50 years – in centenary year, with the Carling Cup in the cabinet and another decent run in Europe under José Mourinho's bullish management.

2. Winning the 1955 title

And being four points clear as we went into the last match of the season at Old Trafford, so United's players and fans were obliged to grit their teeth and sportingly applaud us onto the pitch as champions. Make that Groundhog Day…

3. David Webb's 1970 FA Cup replay-winning header

Hitting the back of the net at Old Trafford (what is it about that place?), in the only final ever to go the full 240 minutes of match, extra time, replay and more extra time. Ron Harris lifted the trophy.

4. The Cup Winners' Cup final Stockholm, 13 May 1998

Gianfranco Zola had barely recovered from a groin injury, but cometh the hour, cometh the man. The little Italian nipped on as a second-half sub against Stuttgart. Seventeen seconds later, with his third touch of the ball, he'd slammed a Dennis Wise pass into the roof of the net for the only goal of the game. Pure magic.

5. Beating Real Madrid 2-1 (3-2 on aggregate) Athens, 21 May 1971

To win the club's first European trophy, the Cup Winners' Cup. The first game, on 19 May, ended 1-1. The replay was staged in the same stadium (it's actually in the port of Piraeus), and hundreds of Chelsea fans who had booked one or two-day travel tours had to sleep rough to see their heroes triumph two nights later.

6. Signing Ruud Gullit 1995
And realising the gloom and uncertainty of the 1980s had given way to an age when achievements would be expected at Stamford Bridge, not greeted with surprise. One megastar attracts others, and Gianfranco Zola, Gianluca Vialli and Marcel Desailly weren't far behind. News of Ruud's move reverberated around the globe as sports editors grasped the fact that Chelsea had entered a thrilling modern era.

7. Beating part-timers Jeunesse Hautcharage of Luxembourg 13-0 1971
The biggest victory in a single European game, with Peter Osgood's tally of eight in the 21-0 aggregate win setting further records. It was one of the wins on the way to Chelsea lifting the Cup Winners' Cup in 1971. Admittedly one of their players only had one arm, but who's counting?

8. Roman Abramovich pitching up in SW6 with his hefty wallet 2004
Better still, he'd looked out of his helicopter window at Tottenham and decided it was a hopeless cause. Mix in José Mourinho's focus and drive, and it seems a winning recipe. The cosy duopoly of Arsenal and Man Utd is shattered, and Blues fans have to pinch themselves every day as the tabloid sports pages link the club with ever more glamorous superstars. Pass the caviar.

9. Chelsea 5 Manchester United 0 3 October 1999
Probably the most satisfying league result in Chelsea's history. United were Premiership champions, FA Cup holders and European Cup holders, and topped the table. Alex Ferguson, that shrewd judge of talent, had splashed out £4.5m on Italian goalie Massimo Taibi to replace Peter Schmeichel. Oh dear. As the goals kept going in, the choruses of "Can we play you every week?" and "Can you play him every week?" left Fergie with a face like thunder. Taibi never played for United again, and the humiliated Ferguson has nursed a grudge against the Blues ever since.

10. Dennis Wise lifting the FA Cup in 2000, one-handed
With his bemused baby son Henry cradled in the other arm. A big 'aaahhhhh' moment for Blues fans. It was the last FA Cup Final under Wembley's Twin Towers, with Roberto Di Matteo scoring the only goal as Chelsea beat Aston Villa 1-0.

11. Leeds United getting relegated 2004
Since the FA Cup final replay victory of 1970, bitter Leeds fans have exulted in any Stamford Bridge disappointments. Not surprisingly, Chelsea fans have reciprocated, so when Leeds flogged their best players and dropped out of the Premiership, there was a collective Blue 'yesssssss!' On the chrome stools of the espresso bars in SW6 they spoke of schadenfreude. In Yorkshire they kicked their whippets.

ALSO PLAYED FOR QPR...

Come to think of it, is there any Chelsea star who hasn't?

1. **Roy Bentley** (1948-56)
2. **Dave Webb** (1968-74)
3. **Ray Wilkins** (1973-79)
4. **Tommy Langley** (1975-80)
5. **Clive Walker** (1975-84)
6. **Mike Fillery** (1978-83)
7. **Nigel Spackman** (1983-89)
8. **Roy Wegerle** (1986-88)
9. **Gavin Peacock** (1993-96) came from Loftus Road
10. **Mark Stein** (1993-98) previously played for QPR
11. **Paul Furlong** (1994-96)

ALTERNATIVE ULSTERS

11 Chelsea players who represented Northern Ireland

1. **Mal Donaghy** 88 caps
2. **Sam Irving** 18 caps
3. **Johnny Kirwan** 17 caps
4. **Billy Mitchell** 15 caps
5. **Billy Dickson** 12 caps
6. **English McConnell** 12 caps
7. **Kevin Wilson** 12 caps
8. **Joe Bambrick** 11 caps
9. **Seamus D'Arcy** 5 caps
10. **Jim Ferris** 5 caps
11. **Tom Priestley** 2 caps

> IN THE ESPRESSO BARS OF SW6 THEY SPOKE OF SCHADENFREUDE. IN LEEDS THEY KICKED THEIR WHIPPETS

AMERICAN PIE

11 who played in the US, for quaintly named teams

1. **Duncan McKenzie** Tulsa Roughnecks
2. **Mickey Thomas** Wichita Wings
3. **Derek Smethurst** San Diego Sockers

4. **Tommy Ord** Rochester Lancers
5. **Charlie Cooke** California Surf
6. **Keith Weller** New England Tea Men
7. **Peter Osgood** Philadelphia Furies
8. **Alan Birchenall** Memphis Rogues
9. **Ian Hamilton** San Jose Earthquakes
10. **Jim McCalliog** Chicago Sting
11. **John Boyle** Tampa Bay Rowdies

AND A GLASS OF WHITE WINE FOR THE LADY?

11 players who served Chelsea, and then behind the bar

1. **Jack Cock** (1919-23) Ran a pub in New Cross.
2. **Reg Williams** (1945-52) Was behind the bar of a local in Bushey, Hertfordshire, and another in Loughton, Essex.
3. **Bill Robertson** (1951-60) Landlord of The Bell at Walton on the Hill after his goalkeeping days were over.
4. **Jim Lewis** (1952-58) Ran a pub near Southend.
5. **Peter Sillett** (1953-62) Mine host of a pub in Ashford, Kent.
6. **Frank Blunstone** (1953-64) Ran two pubs and also managed a wine bar in the Derbyshire market town of Ashbourne.
7. **Terry Venables** (1960-66) Owned the Scribes West nightclub in Kensington.
8. **Bert Murray** (1961-66) Ran a nightclub, but took over a pub in Spalding, Lincs, in 1976 because he didn't like late hours. Over the years he ran four pubs, appropriately in the Stamford area, including The Bull at Market Deeping.
9. **Peter Osgood** (1964-74 and 1978-79) And…
10. **Ian Hutchinson** (1968-76) Ran the Old Union pub in Windsor together. Hutch later managed a pub in Taunton, Somerset.
11. **Steve Kember** (1971-75) Ran a wine bar before returning to coaching.

ANYONE FOR TENNIS?

11 Chelsea players who did well at other sports

1. **Ben Howard Baker** (1921-26)
Played water polo for England.

2. Johnny Jackson (1933-43)
Became a professional golfer, playing in the 1950 Open.
3. Eric Parsons (1950-56)
Was a national bowls player, winning the English singles, pairs and triples.
4. Maxwell Woosnam (1914)
Played Davis Cup tennis for Great Britain.
5. Keith Weller (1970-71)
Flies. Well, he has a pilot's licence, which is sportier than many ex-footballers.
6. Ralph Oelofse (1951-53)
Boxed against the South African middleweight champion, and also once turned down a contract from an American baseball team.
7. John Phillips (1970-80)
Was a keen water-skier.
8. Reginald Weaver (1929-32)
Competed in Edinburgh's famous Powderhall sprints.
9. Mal Donaghy (1992-94)
Played Gaelic football.
10. Clive Allen (1991-92)
Played American football.
11. Arthur Sales (1924-28)
Was a sprinter whose personal best over 100 yards was an impressive 10.5 seconds.

BACK FROM THE BRINK

11 great Chelsea comebacks

1. Chelsea 4 Liverpool 2 26 January 1997
An FA Cup semi-final at Stamford Bridge. Robbie Fowler and Stan Collymore had given Liverpool a comfy 2-0 lead at half-time. Blues manager Ruud Gullit took off Scott Minto and brought on Mark Hughes for the second half, and Sparky scored one, Luca Vialli two and Gianfranco Zola the fourth for an astonishing 4-2 turnaround.

2. Chelsea 3 Vicenza 2 Cup Winners' Cup semi-final, 8 April 1998
It was 2-2 on aggregate with 20 minutes to go in the second leg of the semi-final at Stamford Bridge when Mark Hughes came off the bench. He unleashed a volley that won the tie and helped Chelsea advance to the final and victory over Stuttgart.

3. Chelsea 2 Leeds United 1 FA Cup final replay, 29 April 1970
Arguably the ultimate in comebacks. Chelsea eventually came from behind three times (over the two games, the first ending in a 2-2 draw) to overcome Leeds and lift the trophy in a replayed final at Old Trafford.

4. Chelsea 4 FC Bruges 0 Cup Winners' Cup quarter-final, 24 March 1971
Despite trailing 2-0 from the first leg in Belgium (where Bruges hadn't been beaten in any domestic competition for three years), Chelsea walloped them in the return leg – still regarded by many as one of Chelsea's best team performances of all time. With moments remaining, Chelsea were winning 1-0 but losing 2-1 on aggregate, when Peter Osgood scored to level. In extra time a second goal for Ossie and strikes by Peter Houseman and Tommy Baldwin won the day, en route to lifting the trophy.

5. Blackpool 3 Chelsea 4 24 October 1970
Just 20 minutes remained of this league match at Bloomfield Road, and the Blues'

rookie teenage keeper John Phillips had been beaten three times. But Tommy Baldwin was replaced by winger Charlie Cooke, and defender David Webb was pushed up to join the forwards. Keith Weller struck twice, Webb bagged one, then a Chelsea cross was turned into his own net by Dave Hatton for a last-minute own-goal winner.

6. Chelsea 2 Preston North End 1 FA Cup replay, 3 February 1969
This match took place on a Monday afternoon following a 0-0 draw at Deepdale. The Lilywhites took the lead and held it until the dying moments. Archie Gemmill nearly gave Preston a two-goal lead at the death, beating Peter Bonetti, but he slammed his shot against the bar. Then Preston's keeper blocked David Webb's shot to seemingly cement victory. But with seconds to go, Webb belted a volley home from close range to level. From the restart, Charlie Cooke intercepted a Preston pass and fired home an out-of-the-blue late, late winner.

7. Chelsea 4 Barcelona 2 Champions League, 8 March 2005
After losing 2-1 in the first leg of this knockout tie in Barcelona, Chelsea had it all to do at Stamford Bridge. Three goals (by Eidur Gudjohnsen, Frank Lampard and Damien Duff) in the first 19 minutes of a cracking game appeared to put the result beyond doubt, but two replies by Ronaldinho – one from the spot – gave Barça the away-goals advantage. Then, 14 minutes from the end, captain John Terry rose to head the ball home and clinch a thrilling win 5-4 on aggregate.

8. Chelsea 4 Bolton Wanderers 3 14 October 1978
With barely a quarter of an hour remaining in this Division 1 home game, Chelsea were losing 0-3. On came supersub Clive Walker. He teed up Tommy Langley, then Kenny Swain to bring it back to 2-3, before firing home a glorious equaliser to level at 3-3. In the dying moments, Walker sent a cross into the Bolton area, where future Trotters manager Sam Allardyce unfortunately sliced the ball into his own net to produce a shock 4-3 turnabout.

9. Chelsea 3 Luton Town 3 6 April 1991
Chelsea were already in dire trouble, and losing 0-3 at the Bridge, when Graeme Le Saux was sent off. Yet despite having only ten men, the Blues got their act together and dragged the game back to 3-3 in the dying moments to achieve a result that left manager Bobby Campbell gasping for breath.

10. **Chelsea 3 Derby County 2** 31 December 1910
With six minutes remaining of this New Year's Eve fixture at Stamford Bridge, it was still goalless, and people had started making their way down Fulham Road to the tube. That flow became a tide as Derby's Steve Bloomer converted two spot-kicks to make

it Chelsea 0 Derby 2. But there was more to come. Bob Whittingham pulled one back for respectability, then Angus Douglas fired in a Chelsea equaliser. Finally, in the last remaining seconds, the ref awarded Chelsea a penalty… and Whittingham converted to achieve an improbable win. Moral: wait for the final whistle.

11 Chelsea 6 Newcastle United 5 10 September 1958
With ten minutes to go the Blues were trailing 4-5. Toon keeper Stewart Mitchell played a short goal kick upfield at the precise moment defender Bob Stokoe turned away. The ball struck his rear end and rebounded to Ron Tindall, who stepped forward and scored a late equaliser. Then, as the ref was just about to whistle for full-time, Tindall dived to meet a cross and headed home a remarkable winner.

BAD BOYS

11 Chelsea scandals

1. Dennis Wise once went ape in a cab outside Scribes West, Terry Venables's nightclub. He was arrested and prosecuted. Deafening cries of "Taxi" followed him round Premiership and Championship grounds for years afterwards, especially when taking corners close to opposition fans.

2. In 1936 young Sunderland goalie **James Thorpe** died three days after a tough 3-3 draw with Chelsea at Roker Park. The coroner gave the cause of death as "diabetes accelerated by rough usage received in the match". The fact that Chelsea players were therefore implicated in the fatality provoked waves of recrimination.

3. Mickey Thomas was sentenced to 18 months in prison in 1993 for passing forged £10 notes to trainees at Wrexham, his club at the time. His courtroom jest of "Anyone got change of a tenner for the phone?" might have amused the press, but the judge decided to set an example. Mickey is now a popular after-dinner speaker. Sample quip: "Roy Keane's on 100 grand a week. So was I until the police found my printing machine."

4. Chelsea assistant manager **Graham Rix** was sentenced to a year in Wandsworth in 1999 for having sex with a 15-year-old girl.

5. Chelsea captain **Hughie Gallacher** was cornered by a group of Fulham fans in 1932 in a café after he'd been at the pictures. He got a black eye in the fist fight that resulted, was ordered to put ten shillings in the poor box by West London magistrates (who accepted that there had been some provocation) and was suspended for one match by the club.

6. Teddy Maybank, the blond-haired striker who made his debut for the Blues in 1975, was an early contestant on Cilla Black's *Blind Date*. Not a crime in itself, but he should probably have told his wife that he was heading off for a romantic weekend with the young lady contestant. She didn't see the funny side.

7. In April 1985, without permission from the Football Association or Hammersmith and Fulham Council, **Ken Bates** hired builders to put up 11ft fences round the pitch – topped with barbed wire and electrified wire (although the power was never actually switched on). He based the anti-hooligan fences on the ones used to corral cattle on his farm. It was a move that polarised opinion, with many welcoming the fact that somebody was at last taking firm action against the louts.

8. Alan Birchenall, **Charlie Cooke**, **Peter Osgood** and **John Boyle** – all technically injured – lunched at Barbarella's, the Fulham Road restaurant in the shadow of the old Shed. They shared 14 bottles of wine. Manager **Dave Sexton** went ballistic when the papers got hold of it, and all were dropped for the next match against Southampton. Chelsea lost 5-0.

9. Tommy Baldwin was arrested after throwing a bottle of vodka from a car driven by a man without a licence in a chase involving several police vehicles. The player (torn shirt, blood-stained face) appeared before Old Street magistrates. His eventual four-month jail sentence was suspended on appeal. Baldwin later became the first footballer convicted of drink-driving after the breathalyser was introduced in 1967.

> THE LOGO LOOKED LIKE TWO SQUIGGLES AND A CONTINENTAL SEVEN, HANDWRITTEN BY A CHELSEA PENSIONER

10. John Terry and **Jody Morris** were arrested after a fracas outside the Wellington Club, Knightsbridge, in 2002, after celebrating the birth of Morris's daughter. It threatened to derail Terry's career, especially as it followed an incident in the bar of a Heathrow hotel when he, Morris, **Eidur Gudjohnsen**, **Frank Lampard** and **Frank Sinclair** were fined by the club for drunken trousers-down antics in front of American tourists still in shock at TV coverage of the 9/11 attacks.

11. Having lost 2-0 at Anfield in April 1965, the team stayed in Blackpool ahead of a weekend fixture at Burnley. Three days before the game, eight players broke manager **Tommy Docherty**'s strict curfew and sneaked out for a late-night binge, returning to the hotel at 3am. Tipped off by a porter, a raging Doc pulled back 'sleeping' **John Hollins**'s sheets to reveal him still wearing a jacket and tie. As well as Hollins, the Doc sent **Terry Venables**, **George Graham**, **Eddie McCreadie**, **Barry Bridges**, **Bert Murray**, **Marvin Hinton** and **Joe Fascione** home, drafting in youngsters to take their place. Chelsea were thrashed 6-2. The bitterness lasted years.

BADGES OF DISTINCTION

11 top Chelsea logos

1. 1905-52 Caricature of an octogenarian with bushy white beard. No, it's not Ken Bates, it's a Royal Hospital resident – a Chelsea pensioner complete with medals. Used as the logo on early programmes, it gave rise to the club's original nickname, The Pensioners.

2. 1940s A variation of the old boy in a circular design bearing the name 'The Chelsea Football Club'. Our war hero has shed a few years, ditched the beard and grown bushy side-whiskers.

3. 1952-53 Elaborate CFC motif in a blue shield. The stylised letters, which look like a fish on the move, represent manager Ted Drake's bid to ditch the pensioners tag in favour of the more youthful 'Blues'.

4. 1953-86 Rampant lion with staff, the design that saw Chelsea win the title in 1955 and two cups in the early 1970s. The badge – the first to appear on the shirts – featured the lion from Viscount Chelsea's coat of arms wrapping its paws round the Abbot of Westminster's ornate staff. Round the edge are the club name, two red footballs and three red roses.

5. 1964-66 The lion and staff vanished from the shirts for two years to be replaced with something that looked like two squiggles and a continental seven. It read 'CFC', in what looked like the shaky handwriting of, er, a pensioner.

6. 1970 Winning the FA Cup gave the seamstresses of SW6 a chance to show what they could do. The lion was back, together with a stitched version of the trophy and the date, 1970.

7. 1971 Another year, another trophy, more needlework. The rampant lion and staff were flanked by two gold stars, representing the FA Cup and Cup Winners' Cup.

8. 1986-2005 The lion's still there, but appropriately for the straitened financial circumstances of the club in the 1980s, he's got rid of the staff. Now our roaring blue mascot is clambering over the big bold letters CFC.

9. 1990s variation 1 A colour change. Chelsea players can now legitimately tell the manager they're in the red lion, although in a matter of months it has reverted to blue… with a cutesy little shield around it.

10. 1990s variation 2 Try to keep up. The lion's gone yellow, but now the background is blue.

11. 2005 Back to the future. Based on the design from the 1950s, centenary year is celebrated with a retro lion badge. Thanks to Roman Abramovich's millions, they've re-employed the staff. But it's not a good year for the roses. One flower has gone.

BARBERS' NIGHTMARES

11 Chelsea players who indulged in facial hair

1. **Micky Droy** beard and moustache
2. **Charlie Cooke** moustache
3. **Ian Hutchinson** sideburns you could swing from
4. **John Sparrow** moustache
5. **Gordon Davies** moustache
6. **Kevin Wilson** moustache
7. **Paul Elliott** moustache and beard
8. **Eddie Newton** moustache
9. **Mateja Kezman** beard but no moustache to speak of
10. **Eddie McCreadie** nicotine-stained moustache
11. **Alan Hudson** impressive mutton chops

BATTLES AT THE BRIDGE

11 famous feuds

1. Ruud Gullit v Ken Bates
In the summer of 1998 the player-manager seemed to be stalling over negotiating

a new contract as the expiry date of the old one loomed. Gullit thought his £2m-a-season demand was an initial bargaining position. The Chelsea chairman saw it as an outrageous demand. Despite looming cup finals, Gullit was sacked that February, prompting a bitter war of words, with Bates dubbing Gullit a "part-time playboy manager". The word "netto" entered the language, as Gullit had allegedly been seeking £2m a year after tax.

2. Ken Bates v Matthew Harding

It was all sweetness and light in 1993 when chairman Ken Bates persuaded self-made millionaire and Blues fan Matthew Harding to loan the club £5m, interest-free, to fund the north stand, which still bears his name. But the relationship soured. Bates suspected Harding's friendship with manager Glenn Hoddle was part of a plot to seize control, and the two titans fell out in a bitter war of words and clash of egos. You might have expected Harding's death in a helicopter crash in October 1996 to have ended the acrimony, but Bates continued to refer to Harding as "that bloody megalomaniac".

3. Graeme Le Saux v Robbie Fowler

During an ill-tempered Chelsea v Liverpool league match in February 1999, Fowler and Le Saux had several run-ins. Le Saux (happily married with children) had already endured a barrage of chants from the Liverpool fans, questioning his sexuality. When Fowler turned and provocatively waggled his bum at Le Saux

> "I FELT KERRY DIXON WAS NOT PULLING HIS WEIGHT. IT WAS HANDBAGS AT 40 PACES"

as the Chelsea left-back was about to take a free kick, Le Saux complained to the referee… and was promptly booked for time-wasting. A feud was born.

4. Kerry Dixon v David Speedie

The simmering animosity between the normally placid Dixon and the fiery Scot Speedie exploded into a fist fight in the Stamford Bridge dressing room after a 1-0 defeat by Manchester City in December 1983. "I felt my partner was not pulling his weight, and I was not one to hold back," Speedo later recalled. "It was handbags at 40 paces." The feud didn't last long: indeed the exchange of blows cleared the air. Dixon and Speedie went on to form one of Chelsea's best striking partnerships – in the nicest sense – notching 126 goals in the 145 games they started together.

5. Alan Hudson v Jimmy Hill

In the early 1990s Alan Hudson applied for the vacant managerial post at Fulham – the club he had supported as a boy. Jimmy Hill refused to consider him for the job, according to Hudson, who felt it was a bit rich from the man who "spouted irrelevant nonsense" week after week on the BBC's *Match of the Day*. Hudson alleges Hill had it in for him, refusing to say anything positive about any of his footballing performances when analysing matches on Saturday nights. "He was one of my bitterest enemies," says Hudson. "He never liked me from the time I upstaged him at the Player of the Year awards in 1970. I never had any respect for Hill."

6. Brian Clough v Terry Venables
The Nottingham Forest manager hated Chelsea, and Terry Venables in particular. No one is entirely sure when or where the loathing started, but Clough always referred to the Blues as "spivs", and regarded Terry Venables as the personification of everything that was bad about flashy modern football in west London. When Chelsea racked up a string of victories over Forest, Clough's hatred deepened – if such a thing were possible.

7. Ken Bates v Graham Roberts
Robbo signed for Chelsea in August 1988, but Bates and Roberts never hit it off. Enraged at something Bates had said or done, Roberts went to the Football Association and alleged he had been given an illegal £100,000 payment by Bates to buy a house in Scotland, and that he had been promised other illegal payments. He also alleged other Chelsea players had been given illegal payments. Bates and Chelsea deny the allegations to this day… but the FA sided with Robbo, and fined Chelsea a then record £105,000.

8. Chelsea v Leeds United
The clubs, and their respective supporters, have hated each other for decades. Leeds see Chelsea as southern softies, Chelsea see Leeds as northern thugs. No quarter was given in matches between the clubs in the 1960s, with Ron Harris and Norman Hunter leading the action for their respective clans. When Chelsea beat Leeds in the 1970 FA Cup final replay, it stoked a feud which continues to this day.

9. Chelsea v Mike Kelly
Queen's Park Rangers goalie Mike Kelly failed Peter Osgood on a coaching course in the late 1960s. As luck would have it, Chelsea promptly drew QPR at Loftus Road in the 1970 FA Cup quarter-final. In a match already spiced up by the presence in the Rangers side of ex-Blues Terry Venables and Barry Bridges, Ossie scored a hat-trick in a 4-2 win. As the third goal hit the back of the net, Osgood walked up to Kelly and said: "Stick to f**king coaching!" A quarter of a century later the war continued. Kelly – then Middlesbrough goalkeeping coach – came to the Bridge with his new team… and got into a scuffle in the tunnel with Alan Hudson, 'representing' the Chelsea team of 1970, who had been making a half-time presentation on the pitch.

10. Chelsea v UEFA

After the first round of Chelsea's epic 2005 Champions League battle against Barcelona, José Mourinho claimed he had seen Barça manager Frank Rijkaard enter referee Anders Frisk's dressing room at half-time, to influence the man-in-black's decision-making in the second half. Mourinho later backtracked slightly, conceding he hadn't personally witnessed the incident. Mourinho and Chelsea were together fined £40,000, and the Blues manager was given a two-match touchline ban. A prevalent feeling was that Chelsea, backed by Abramovich's billions, were starting to see themselves as more powerful than European football's governing body. However, facts later emerged that went some way towards vindicating Mourinho.

11. Ken Bates v the press

The former Chelsea chairman took exception to any criticism of his methods, or club, in the tabloids, and regularly banned individual journalists. His column in the matchday programme was eagerly turned to, not least by journalists themselves, for whom a slagging off by Ken was deemed a worthy badge of honour. Indeed, not to be mentioned almost suggested that hacks weren't doing their job properly.

BEYOND THE SEA

Chelsea's first 11 overseas players

1. **Nils Middelboe** (Denmark) 1913-21
2. **Willi Steffen** (Switzerland) 1946-47
3. **Frank Mitchell** (Australia) 1949-52
4. **Ralph Oelofse** (South Africa) 1951-53
5. **Tony Potrac** (South Africa) 1970-73
6. **Derek Smethurst** (South Africa) 1971
7. **Petar Borota** (Yugoslavia) 1979-82
8. **Colin Viljoen** (South Africa) 1980-82
9. **Tony Dorigo** (Australia) 1987-91
10. **David Mitchell** (Australia) 1988-91
11. **Ken Monkou** (The Netherlands) 1989-92

BIG MACS

11 Scottish sons of Chelsea

1. Eddie McCreadie
2. Jim McCalliog
3. Kevin McAllister
4. Tony McAndrew
5. Ian MacFarlane
6. Duncan McKenzie
7. Joe McLaughlin
8. Errol McNally
9. John McNaught
10. Bobby McNeil
11. John McNichol

BLACK AND BLUE

Chelsea's first 11 black players

1. Paul Canoville
2. Keith Jones
3. Keith Dublin
4. Clive Wilson
5. Ken Monkou
6. Andy Myers
7. Frank Sinclair
8. Paul Elliott
9. Eddie Newton
10. Mark Stein
11. Paul Furlong

BLOND BOMBSHELLS

11 Chelsea players who had more fun

1. Chris Garland
2. Ken Shellito
3. Jim Thompson

4. Steve Sherwood
5. Steve Wicks
6. Joe Allon
7. Clive Walker
8. Tore Andre Flo
9. Mikael Forssell
10. Graeme Le Saux
11. Eidur Gudjohnsen

BOOT-BOY ANTHEMS

11 Chelsea chants from the Shed

1. We're the middle, we're the middle, we're the middle of the Shed!
Each part of the Shed tried to outsing the other, before all three sections came together in the final chorus.
We're the middle, we're the middle, we're the middle of the Shed!
We're the west side, we're the west side, we're the west side of the Shed!
We're the white wall, we're the white wall, we're the white wall of the Shed!
We're the Sh-e-ed, we're the Sh-e-ed, we're the Shed at Stamford Bridge.

2. The Chelsea Shed is colourful
To the tune: *When the Saints Go Marching In.*
The Chelsea Shed is colourful
The Chelsea Shed is colourful
Full of boots, full of bottles, full of razors
The Chelsea Shed is colourful.

> WHEN EVERYBODY AT THE BACK OF THE SHED SURGED, YOU'D FIND YOURSELF 30FT DOWN THE TERRACES

3. Knees up Mother Brown, knees up Mother Brown
The song which accompanied alarming 'surges' in the Shed, when you'd suddenly find yourself 30ft down the terraces as everybody pushed forward from the back.
Knees up Mother Brown, knees up Mother Brown
Under the table you must go, ee-aye-ee-aye-ee-aye-o,
If I catch you bending, I'll saw your legs right off
Knees up, knees up, don't get the breeze up,
Knees up Mother Brown!
Oh, my, what a rotten song
What a rotten song, what a rotten song,

Oh my, what a rotten song
What a rotten singer too!

4. Tottenham sing, I don't know why

To the tune: *Tom Hark.*
Tottenham sing, I don't know why
Cos after the match, you're gonna die.

5. If you're standing on the corner

To the tune: *The Liver Birds* theme.
If you're standing on the corner
With a red scarf round your neck
Chelsea boys'll come and get ya
And we'll break your f**king neck
Na, na, na, nah, na, na, na, nah…

6. I was born under the Chelsea Shed

To the tune: *Wand'rin' Star.*
I was born under the Chelsea Shed
I was born under the Chelsea Shed
Knives are made for stabbing
Guns are made to shoot
If you come down the Chelsea Shed
We'll all stick in the boot…

7. Harry Roberts is my friend

To the tune: *London Bridge is Falling Down.*
Harry Roberts is my friend
Is my friend, is my friend,
Harry Roberts is my friend
He kills coppers
A chant to wind up police threading their way into the Shed to make arrests. Harry Roberts shot three policemen dead in Shepherd's Bush – two miles from the Bridge.

8. Chelsea boot boys!

To the tune: *Na Na, Hey Hey, Kiss Him Goodbye*, by Steam – and, later, Bananarama.
Na, na, na, na. Na, na, na, na,
Hey-ey-ey
Chelsea boot boys!

9. Boots wrapped round your head
To the tune: The Gap Band's *Oops Upside your Head*.
Boots wrapped round your head
I said, boots wrapped round your head!

10. We had joy, we had fun
To the tune: *Seasons In The Sun*.
We had joy
We had fun
We had Luton on the run
But the fun didn't last
Cos the bastards ran too fast!

11. If you go down to the Shed today
To the tune: *Teddy Bears' Picnic*.

If you go down to the Shed today
You're sure of a big surprise
If you go down to the Shed today
You'll never believe your eyes
For Jeremy, the Sugar Puffs bear
Has bought his boots and cropped his hair
And now he's off to join the Chelsea skinheads

BOX TO BOX

11 Chelsea players who became pundits

1. **Graeme Le Saux** BBC
2. **John Hollins** Sky
3. **Gavin Peacock** BBC
4. **Andy Townsend** ITV
5. **Nigel Spackman** Sky
6. **Ray Wilkins** BBC
7. **Mickey Thomas** phone-in host for Manchester's Century Radio
8. **Paul Elliott** Channel 4
9. **Jakob Kjeldberg** Danish TV
10. **George Graham** PremPlus
11. **Clive Allen** 5Live and ITV

BRAVEHEARTS

11 Chelsea players who represented Scotland

1. **Bobby Evans** 48 caps
2. **Pat Nevin** 28 caps
3. **Tommy Docherty** 25 caps
4. **Eddie McCreadie** 23 caps
5. **Hughie Gallacher** 20 caps
   Tommy Walker 20 caps
7. **Alex Jackson** 17 caps
8. **Charlie Cooke** 16 caps
   John Tait Robertson 16 caps
10. **Derek Johnstone** 14 caps
11. **George Graham** 12 caps
    Andy Wilson 12 caps

BROLLIES, BOTTLES AND BOUQUETS

11 unusual objects associated with Chelsea FC

1. An umbrella
When John Dempsey was playing in an international for the Republic of Ireland in Norway, the ball went out of play. As he stooped to retrieve it, an old woman hit him over the head with her brolly.

2. A bottle of Heinz Salad Cream
Dave Beasant dropped one on his right foot while making a sandwich at home, severing the tendons on his big toe. He was on crutches for two months.

3. Eleven bouquets of flowers
In a rather touching post-war gesture of comradeship, the players of Moscow Dynamo presented each Chelsea player with a bouquet before their match at Stamford Bridge in November 1945. The embarrassed boys in blue quickly passed them on to the ballboys for safekeeping, and they were placed in the tap room, next to the changing rooms. Then they were all stolen during the game.

4. An earring
As a condition of joining the board, Matthew Harding insisted that if Chelsea reached the FA Cup final, Ken Bates would wear an earring in the Royal Box. Ken did.

5. A beer bottle
John Boyle was knocked out by a beer bottle thrown by an AS Roma fan before the Inter-Cities Fairs Cup match in Italy in October 1965.

6. A 50p piece
Mateja Kezman was struck in the face by a coin thrown by a West Ham lout in the FA Cup third round match at the Bridge in October 2004. It narrowly missed his eye.

7. A stick of celery
Jamie Oliver may want us to crunch more of the stuff, but in the 1980s stewards frisked fans at the turnstiles to confiscate illicit items of salad. The ban followed a rash of celery-related injuries as fans flung the contents of the North End Road's market stalls around the terraces while chanting an appropriate ditty. See Singing The Blues for full lyrics. Celery is still thrown to celebrate trophies.

8. A dog lead
Carlo Cudicini tweaked his knee while walking his dog in the summer of 2001. It required a minor operation. The knee, not the dog.

9. A railway ticket from Paddington station
Ken Bates used to dispense them. His first job was as a clerk in the ticket office there.

10. A champagne bottle
Before Gianluca Vialli's first game as manager in 1998 he gathered the team together in the dressing room and poured everyone a glass of bubbly.

11. A rugby scrum cap
Tom Priestly, an inside-forward in the 1930s, always wore one on the pitch because of a childhood illness which made his hair fall out.

CHAPPI, SPARKY AND THE SPONGE

11 players' nicknames

1. Berge Graeme Le Saux (after fellow Jerseyman Bergerac).

2. Starsky Garry Stanley (although his career barely overlapped with Hutch).

3. Chopper Ron Harris (because of his tendency to scythe down opponents).

4. Jukebox Gordon Durie (after *Jukebox Jury*, the TV show of the 1960s in which celebrities passed a "hit" or "miss" verdict on new pop releases).

5. The Sponge Tommy Baldwin (because of his phenomenal drinking powers, especially when stuck in a bar with Charlie Cooke).

6. Bolo Boudewijn Zenden (fewer Scrabble points but much easier to pronounce).

7. Chappi Albert Ferrer (his nickname at Barcelona. It's Spanish slang for bottle top, and refers to the diminutive right-back's size.)

8. Sparky Mark Hughes (for his firecracker shots and matchday temperament. TV commentator Brian Moore once memorably said: "Mark Hughes; Sparky by name, Sparky by nature. The same can be said of Brian McClair!")

9. Gatling Gun George Hilsdon (for his astonishing firing rate).

10. The Cat Peter Bonetti (a nickname bestowed by early playing colleague Ron Tindall because of his grace, balance and handling skills).

11. The Rabbit Eric Parsons (for his sprinting ability down the wing).

CHELSEA REJECTS
11 defectors to hated rivals

1. **Gus Poyet** to Tottenham Hotspur
2. **Michael Duberry** to Leeds United
3. **Ray Wilkins** to Manchester United
4. **Terry Venables** to Tottenham Hotspur
5. **George Graham** to Arsenal
6. **Jason Cundy** to Tottenham Hotspur
7. **Derek Smethurst** to Millwall
8. **Jimmy Greaves** to Tottenham (via AC Milan)
9. **Mike Fillery** to QPR
10. **Gordon Durie** to Tottenham Hotspur
11. **Tony Dorigo** to Leeds United

COME ON YOU, ER, REDS
11 Chelsea players and the teams they supported as boys

1. **Clive Walker** Manchester United
2. **Kevin Wilson** Leeds United
3. **Vinnie Jones** Watford
4. **Frank Sinclair** Liverpool
5. **Andy Myers** QPR
6. **Graham Stuart** Southampton
7. **Ken Monkou** Feyenoord
8. **Alan Hudson** Fulham
9. **Pat Nevin** Celtic
10. **Mark Hughes** Chelsea
11. **Tony Cascarino** Millwall

DEBUTANT'S BALLS

Around 80 players have scored on their debuts for Chelsea. Here are 11 of them

1. **James Robertson** 1905
2. **George Hilsdon** scored five on his debut, 1906
3. **James Bradshaw** 1909
4. **Seamus O'Connell** scored a hat-trick on his debut, 1954
5. **Peter Osgood** 1965
6. **John Boyle** 1965
7. **Nigel Spackman** 1983
8. **Joe Allon** 1991
9. **Mick Harford** 1992
10. **Gavin Peacock** 1993
11. **Paul Furlong** 1994

DISTANT RELATIONS

11 other Chelseas

1. Chelsea Clinton
Daughter of the sax-blowing ex-US president.

2. Chelsy Davy
Zimbabwe-born blonde tipped to wed Prince Harry.

3. Chelsea Hotel
Famously bohemian New York hotel where punk icon Sid Vicious killed his girlfriend Nancy before taking his own life.

4. Chelsea Flower Show
Upmarket event in the grounds of the Royal Hospital, home to the Pensioners.

5. Chelsea Girl
Teen fashion shop chain of the 1960 and 1970s, later reinvented as River Island.

6. Chelsea, Maine
New England town (pop 2,627) in the Kennebec Valley. Other Chelseas include
examples in Suffolk County, Massachusetts; Vermont; Victoria, Australia...

7. Chelsea Drugstore
The King's Road bar immortalised in the Rolling Stones song *You Can't Always Get
What You Want*. Now a McDonald's.

8. Chelsea tractor
Derogatory nickname for four-wheel-drive urban gas-guzzlers.

9. Chelsea Girls
Andy Warhol's first cinema success in 1966 was partly shot at the Chelsea Hotel.
Six-and-a-half hours of unscripted, improvised action by lesbians, sado-masochists
and hustler queens... much like Fulham Road on Friday nights.

10. Chelsea boots
Gentlemen's elastic-sided ankle-length footwear.

11. Chelsea clip
Hooked security device (£2.55 plus VAT) screwed to the underside of tables in
Sloane Square cafes to thwart bag-snatchers.

DOCS, DRAKES AND JOSÉ MOURINHO

11 all-time greatest managers

1. José Mourinho 2004-
No doubt about it. The Portuguese coach with the laser beam stare and famous grey
overcoat tops the list after scooping the league title and Carling Cup in his first
season, 2004/05, after the club's 50-year wait for the game's most treasured piece of
silverware. With a self-belief bordering on arrogance (despite never having played
the game professionally), Mourinho has funnelled Roman Abramovich's billions into

developing a young side with the potential to dominate English football for years to come. Missing out on a place in the 2005 Champions League final after losing 1-0 to Liverpool at Anfield in the second leg of the semis has merely made the ex-Porto manager more determined to achieve glory with Chelsea.

2. Ted Drake 1952-61
He collected three champions' medals with Arsenal in the late 1930s (scoring 42 goals in 1934/35) before taking charge at Chelsea and leading his 'Ducklings' to the league title in 1955. Drake was blessed with a brilliant back-up team who helped develop an active youth policy, founded in 1947 under the curious code name Tudor Rose, that spawned Jimmy Greaves, Terry Venables, Ron Harris and Peter Bonetti. The pundits sneered when he signed several amateur players and Third Division cast-offs to play in the first team, but the man who shook each player's hand and wished them "All the best" as they took the pitch, knew committed footballers when he saw them, and had the last laugh when they played their way to Division 1 glory.

3. Gianluca Vialli 1998-2000
Won more items of silverware than he could carry after helping Chelsea lift the 1998 League Cup, 1998 Cup Winners' Cup, 1998 European Super Cup and 2000 FA Cup. Having shocked the football world by appointing him in place of Ruud Gullit, chairman Ken Bates sat back with a satisfied smile as trophy after trophy found its way to the Blues' otherwise dusty cabinet. Vialli continued the process of moulding Chelsea's overseas stars into the successful unit that Gullit had envisaged. His signings included Marcel Desailly and Gianfranco Zola – both good enough reasons to justify his high position in the managerial hall of fame. Was spectacularly sacked after five disappointing games at the start of the 2000/1 season.

> THE CLUB'S YOUTH POLICY IN THE TED DRAKE YEARS WAS ODDLY CODENAMED TUDOR ROSE

4. Dave Sexton 1967-74
Managed Leyton Orient, Fulham and Arsenal before returning to Stamford Bridge – where he'd been a coach in the mid-60s – to steer the club through one of its golden eras. To be fair, he inherited a brilliant squad from the departing Tommy Docherty. In 1970 Chelsea finished third in the league and lifted the FA Cup, while the following season saw victory in the Cup Winners' Cup. The quiet man of football management proved he had a real flair for cup competitions, but later fell out with several of the club's top stars, including Peter Osgood. This, coupled with financial pressure incurred by the building of the expensive East Stand, eventually led to his departure.

11 DUCKLINGS: TED DRAKE'S TITLE-WINNING SIDE OF 1955

Bill Robertson

Peter Sillett   Stan Willemse

Ron Greenwood   Ken Armstrong

Derek Saunders

Jim Lewis

Eric Parsons   Les Stubbs

John McNichol   Roy Bentley

Manager Ted Drake drafted in amateurs and Third Division cast-offs, and the 'Ducklings' won the league 50 years after Chelsea's creation.

5. Ruud Gullit 1996-98

The dreadlocked one took over from Glenn Hoddle and used his clout, reputation and charisma to enlist Luca Vialli, Frank Leboeuf and Roberto Di Matteo to the cause, pledging a commitment to sexy football. He won the FA Cup by beating Middlesbrough 2-0 in 1997, generating thousands of pounds in sales of replica wigs on the matchday stalls along Fulham Road. But talks over a contract renewal broke down, with chairman Ken Bates accusing Gullit of greed, while Gullit countered that he had merely been adopting a tough initial negotiating stance. Either way, it paved the path for Vialli to reap the benefits of the team Gullit had assembled.

6. Tommy Docherty 1961-67

The much-travelled Doc, who famously claimed to have had more clubs than Jack Nicklaus, arrived as Chelsea were relegated to the old Division 2. His inspired youth policy paved the way for the glory days of the early 1970s, and the Blues were soon back in the top flight and on their way to victory in the League Cup in 1965. Despite reaching several cup semi-finals, it eventually took a much milder character in Dave Sexton (Docherty's former chief scout) to get the best out of the so-called Diamonds. There's no denying that it was an exciting time to watch football at the Bridge.

7. Claudio Ranieri 2000-04

An affable and astute manager who'd guided Cagliari from the Italian Third Division to the top flight, steered Fiorentina into Serie A and won the 1999 Spanish Cup with Valencia, the Tinkerman joined Chelsea in September 2000 as a replacement for compatriot Gianluca Vialli. Famous for his curious but very quotable pidgin English pronouncements, he paved the way for the José Mourinho era after weathering the storm of derision from the experts who reckoned £11m was an absurd amount to pay for West Ham midfielder Frank Lampard in June 2001.

8. Glenn Hoddle 1993-96

The former Tottenham wizard arrived with a pledge to produce a team that specialised in attractive football. Under Hoddle, Chelsea again found themselves playing European matches, but the call from his country was too strong, and Hoddle took over as England manager. Before he went, he generously said:"Managing Chelsea is without doubt the proudest moment in my football career." Arguably the finest thing he did was sign his eventual successor, Ruud Gullit, in a bid to create a side with truly continental flair. He also signed Mark Hughes, which has rankled with Manchester United fans ever since. Hoddle's biggest disappointment was losing the 1994 FA Cup final 4-0 to 'Manure'.

9. John Tait Robertson 1905-6

Chelsea's first manager, a canny Scottish half-back with 16 caps, helped steamroller a club with a big ground but no players straight into the Football League. He then built a squad of established professionals (including monster goalie Willie Foulke), lured to Stamford Bridge by the capital's bright lights. Jackie, as he was known, narrowly missed taking Chelsea to promotion to the top flight in his first season, but his exciting all-star team gelled remarkably quickly and pulled in crowds of up to 67,000. Canny manager getting his stars to gel quickly? Hmm. Sounds familiar…

10. David Calderhead 1907-33

In an era when five years seems a long time for a manager to remain in his post, 26 years is boggling. Calderhead was signed by the board after guiding Lincoln City to an FA Cup draw and replay defeat against the Blues. Although he didn't win a trophy in his quarter of a century at the helm, he took the side to the 1915 FA Cup final and signed legends Hughie Gallacher and Alex James in 1930. Longevity and stability deserve rewards, although six of his 26 seasons were spent in Division 2.

11. Geoff Hurst 1979-81

It could be argued that even the tea lady would have been better than Danny Blanchflower, who had mismanaged the Blues for less than a year. England's 1966

World Cup hero took the reins with Chelsea mired in Division 2 mediocrity, and within weeks Chelsea were top of the table. They just missed out on a promotion place on that occasion, but in Hurst's second season Chelsea endured their bleakest spell in the club's history, scoring just two goals in 13 games. Hurst had to go.

DONNING THE GLOVES

11 emergency goalkeepers

1. David Webb 26 December 1971, Chelsea 2 Ipswich Town 0
Arguably Chelsea's most versatile player of all time, the 6ft defender was regularly emergency striker (33 goals) as well as emergency keeper. Ipswich must have hated the sight of him. On Boxing Day 1968, as part of a makeshift front line, he scored a hat-trick at Portman Road. When Ipswich visited the Bridge on Boxing Day three years later, Webby made his goalkeeping debut at the age of 25. He kept a clean sheet in front of 44,000 delirious fans, so technically enjoys a 100 per cent record.

2. David Speedie 19 March 1986, Chelsea 1 QPR 1
Eddie Niedzwiecki severely injured his knee in the Division 1 match at Stamford Bridge, and was replaced by Speedo. Chelsea were 1-0 up at the time, but Rangers sub David Kerslake scored with a long-distance lob to level. To be fair to Speedie, he wasn't the tallest makeshift keeper in football history.

3. Vinnie Jones various
The notoriously aggressive midfielder relished pulling on the green jersey in times of crisis, and was called upon a couple of times when keepers were injured. Bizarrely – though not totally surprisingly, given the unpredictability of the man – he was once booked for time-wasting in goal, even though Chelsea were 3-0 down.

4. Glen Johnson FA Cup, 20 February 2005, Newcastle United 1 Chelsea 0
The Blues were already down to 10 men in this 5th-round tie when Wayne Bridge had to be stretchered off with a broken ankle. All three substitutes had already been used in a bold triple reshuffle, so when Carlo Cudicini was red-carded, Johnson seized the initiative. Despite the snow swirling around St James' Park, he insisted the dismissed keeper take off his goalie's shirt in the middle of the pitch, then made one excellent save in the dying seconds, blocking a ferocious 25-yard shot.

5. Robert Mackie FA Cup, 2 September 1905, Southend United 0 Chelsea 1
With colossus Willie Foulke and reserve keeper Micky Byrne both unavailable,

right-back Bob Mackie volunteered. He kept a clean sheet on his only appearance between the posts in three seasons at the club.

6. Reg Williams FA Cup, 29 January 1949, Chelsea 2 Everton 0
When keeper Peter Pickering had to leave the field to have stitches in a head wound, wing-half Williams donned the jersey and kept a clean sheet until Pickering was able to come back on, heavily bandaged. Our hero, who played for Chelsea between 1945 and 1952, then went back to his usual position, ran upfield and scored to help Chelsea win the game.

7. Ron Tindall 27 August 1958, Chelsea 4 Tottenham 2
Ron had already scored twice to give Chelsea a comfortable lead when duty called. After half-an-hour's play in this midweek home game, goalie Reg Matthews collided with Spurs' Bobby Smith and was stretchered off. Ron took over. For 20 minutes he denied Spurs, then Smith beat him to make the score 2-1. However, Matthews came back on during the second half, and Jimmy Greaves immediately extended Chelsea's lead on the way to an exciting 4-2 victory.

8. Bert Murray 24 March 1962, Chelsea 2 Arsenal 3
When Peter Bonetti dislocated his elbow during a league match at Stamford Bridge, 'Ruby' was his makeshift replacement. Sadly for Bert, Chelsea lost.

9. Tommy Langley 10 March 1979, Norwich City 2 Chelsea 0
Petar Borota suffered a gashed forehead at Carrow Road and while he was off having eight stitches in the wound, Tommy Langley took over. Chelsea were already one down. Langley pulled off a few good saves, but a second goal by Martin Peters clinched the win for the Canaries.

10. John Coady various
The right-back, who played for the Blues in the late 1980s, was occasionally called upon to step into the breach.

11. Harry Ford various
One of the longest-serving players for Chelsea (1912-24), the No 7 used to take over in goal if James Molyneux was hurt.

DON'T FANCY YOURS MUCH

The 11 ugliest Chelsea players

1. Ed de Goey
Buck-toothed, balding, double-chinned circus freak.

2. Micky Droy
Disfigured caveman. Mind you, you wouldn't say it to his face.

3. Tony Hateley
Hatchet-faced bodyguard from a third-rate gangster movie.

4. Gianfranco Zola
A lovely guy, but he looked like he'd gone through the windscreen in a pile-up and had his face rebuilt by a surgeon wearing metal gloves.

5. Mick Harford
Like a block of grim 1960s housing on legs.

6. Marco Ambrosio
Looked like he'd been hit by Eurostar.

7. Vinnie Jones
Roadkill shrew. Unless he's reading this, in which case he looks like a dashing Hollywood pin-up.

8. Doug Rougvie
Like the loser in a heavyweight bout that's gone the whole distance.

9. Michael Duberry
How a Malteser would look if it was placed under a hot grill.

10. Joe Allon
Child's drawing of Bugs Bunny... with psoriasis.

11. Craig Burley
When he took his false teeth out he looked like the evil crone from a child's nightmare.

FAMOUS FANS

11 celebrities, past and present, in the stands

1. **Damon Albarn** of Blur and Gorillaz
2. **John Major**, the Currie-loving ex-PM
3. **Dennis Waterman**, the actor
4. **Alan Price**, keyboard player of The Animals and his own Set
5. **Princess Margaret** (who confided "I hope you win" to captain Ron Harris before the 1970 FA Cup final)
6. **Rodney Bewes** of the *Likely Lads*
7. **Tom Courtenay** actor (a Hull City fan who adopted Chelsea as his 'London club')
8. **Alec Stewart**, the cricketer
9. **Suggs** from Madness
10. **Michael Crawford**, the actor
11. **Richard O'Sullivan**, the actor

FANCY DANS

11 Chelsea players who fancied themselves in the arts

1. Gianfranco Zola
Plays the piano. "I like Elton John," he once admitted.

2. Jack Cock
Top scorer in the 1919/20 season, the tenor regularly sang on stage at the Walham Green Music Hall. Also played the lead in the 1930s football film *The Great Game*.

3. Terry Venables
Always fancied his abilities as a crooner, especially after a couple of glasses.

Regularly hopped up on stage at Hammersmith Palais to regale punters with numbers such as *Come Fly With Me*. Never turned down a chance to sing at his nightclub, Scribes West.

4. David Webb
Another crooner. Once recorded a version of *Alouette*.

5. Petar Borota
Couldn't sing particularly well, but he was an accomplished artist, painting in oils and exhibiting his work in a London gallery in the spring of 1980.

6. Alan Birchenall
Sang on stage with Joe Cocker in his youth.

7. Joe Cole
Is learning the guitar.

8. Jakob Kjeldbjerg
Would entertain friends with renditions of Bee Gees songs on the piano.

9. Peter Osgood
Once recorded a version of Middle of the Road's hit *Chirpy Chirpy, Cheep Cheep*.

10. Peter Lee Stirling and Daniel Boone
They created *Blue is the Colour*, which became the first football club Top Ten hit, reaching No 5 in 1972. Each player received £300 – about two weeks' pay – for his work. Later Chelsea squads had mixed success with *No One Can Stop Us Now* and *Blue Day* (featuring Suggs) – the only hit to include the word 'albeit', as in the excruciating rhyme "*We've got some memories, albeit from the 70s*".

11. Ruud Gullit
Played bass guitar and bongos for the reggae band Revelation Time.

Not sure if it counts as artistic endeavour, but Peter Bonetti led the England 1970 World Cup squad in a rendition of Lily The Pink – and that's where his World Cup peaked.

> EL TEL NEVER TURNED DOWN A CHANCE TO BREAK INTO "COME FLY WITH ME" AT HIS LONDON NIGHTCLUB

FAVOURITE LEAGUE TABLE NO.1

League Division 1 1954/5

	P	W	D	L	F	A	W	D	L	F	A	Pts
1. Chelsea	42	11	5	5	43	29	9	7	5	38	28	52
2. Wolverhampton Wanderers	42	13	5	3	58	30	6	5	10	31	40	48
3. Portsmouth	42	13	5	3	44	21	5	7	9	30	41	48
4. Sunderland	42	8	11	2	39	27	7	7	7	25	27	48
5. Manchester United	42	12	4	5	44	30	8	3	10	40	44	47
6. Aston Villa	42	11	3	7	38	31	9	4	8	34	42	47
7. Manchester City	42	11	5	5	45	36	7	5	9	31	33	46
8. Newcastle United	42	12	5	4	53	27	5	4	12	36	50	43
9. Arsenal	42	12	3	6	44	25	5	6	10	25	38	43
10. Burnley	42	11	3	7	29	19	6	6	9	22	29	43
11. Everton	42	9	6	6	32	24	7	4	10	30	44	42
12. Huddersfield Town	42	10	4	7	28	23	4	9	8	35	45	41
13. Sheffield United	42	10	3	8	41	34	7	4	10	29	52	41
14. Preston North End	42	8	5	8	47	33	8	3	10	36	31	40
15. Charlton Athletic	42	8	6	7	43	34	7	4	10	33	41	40
16. Tottenham Hotspur	42	9	4	8	42	35	7	4	10	30	38	40
17. West Bromwich Albion	42	11	5	5	44	33	5	3	13	32	63	40
18. Bolton Wanderers	42	11	6	4	45	29	2	7	12	17	40	39
19. Blackpool	42	8	6	7	33	26	6	4	11	27	38	38
20. Cardiff City	42	9	4	8	41	38	4	7	10	21	38	37
21. Leicester City	42	9	6	6	43	32	3	5	13	31	54	35
22. Sheffield Wednesday	42	7	7	7	42	38	1	3	17	21	62	26

FEWEST CLEAN SHEETS IN A LEAGUE SEASON

And the keepers who got backache picking the ball out of the net

1. **One** 1960/61, Peter Bonetti and Reg Matthews
2. **Four** 1990/91, Dave Beasant and Kevin Hitchcock
3. **Five** 1958/59 , Reg Matthews and William Robertson
   Five 1959/60, Reg Matthews, William Robertson and Peter Bonetti
   Five 1978/79, Peter Bonetti, Petar Borota, Robert Iles and John Phillips
6. **Six** 1909/10, Jack Whitley, Arthur Robinson and James Saunders
   Six 1914/15, James Molyneux and Colin Hampton
   Six 1932/33, Victor Woodley

Six 1935/36, Victor Woodley and Johnny Jackson
Six 1938/39, Victor Woodley
Six 1948/49, Harry Medhurst and Peter Pickering
Six 1949/50, Harry Medhurst and Peter Pickering
Six 1953/54, William Robertson, Charles Thomson and Michael Collins
Six 1974/75, John Phillips and Peter Bonetti

FEWEST GOALSCORERS IN A LEAGUE SEASON

11 shot-shy seasons

1. **Seven** 1938/39
2. **Eight** 1908/09
   Eight 1967/68
4. **Nine** 1936/37
   Nine 1949/50
   Nine 1953/54
7. **Ten** 1907/08
   Ten 1914/15
   Ten 1933/34
   Ten 1961/62
   Ten 1968/69
   Ten 1969/70

FEWEST LEAGUE GOALS CONCEDED

The 11 seasons when Chelsea's defence stood firmest

1. **2004/05** 15 goals
2. **1998/99** 30 goals
   2003/04 30 goals
4. **1906/07** 34 goals
   1911/12 34 goals
   1999/2000 34 goals
7. **1910/11** 35 goals
8. **1905/06** 37 goals
   1924/25 37 goals
10. **2001/02** 38 goals
    2002/03 38 goals

11 FIRST 11: THE FIRST CHELSEA TEAM

The team which lost 1-0 at Stockport County on Saturday 2 September 1905. To get the team in formation, we've ditched first names. For the record the team was Willie Foulke, Robert Mackie, Robert McEwan, George Key, Bob McRoberts, Tommy Miller, Martin Moran, John Tait Robertson, David Copeland, Jimmy Windridge, John Kirwan.

FEWEST LEAGUE GOALS SCORED

The 11 seasons when other clubs' defences stood firmest

1. **1923/24** 31 goals
2. **1921/22** 40 goals
3. **1974/75** 42 goals
4. **1978/79** 44 goals
5. **1922/23** 45 goals
6. **1913/14** 46 goals
   1977/78 46 goals
   1980/81 46 goals
   1995/96 46 goals
10. **1909/10** 47 goals
11. **1920/21** 48 goals

FINGERS CROSSED

11 Chelsea superstitions

1. Michael Duberry and Frank Sinclair
Both insisted on a brand new pair of socks for every game.

2. Roberto di Matteo
Refused to have his kit hanging from a peg, like everyone else's. He insisted on his shirt, shorts and socks being placed on the floor.

3. Alan Hudson
Consulted a medium in Victoria ahead of the 1970 FA Cup final. She informed him that he wouldn't score at Wembley. "She was right," said Hudson later. "But she didn't tell me I wouldn't play!" Just before the game, Huddy damaged his ligaments and not only missed the Wembley match, but the Old Trafford replay as well.

4. Peter Houseman
Refused to drive his Vauxhall Viva estate car to games because of a pre-match superstition. Peter Bonetti or John Hollins used to drive it for him. By a tragic twist of fate, Houseman and his wife were killed in a head-on collision two years after he left.

5. David Webb, Ian Hutchinson and Charlie Cooke
All three refused to have haircuts as long as Chelsea kept winning in the 1970 FA Cup in case it proved unlucky.

6. Juan Sebastian Veron
Wears a bandage on his right knee as a kind of amulet. He doesn't need it, but keeps it there for superstitious reasons after once injuring the knee playing for Sampdoria.

7. Ed de Goey
Insisted on having his pre-match rub before any other player.

8. Dennis Wise
Always wore the same 'lucky' vest under his shirt, even when it became tatty.

9. George Hilsdon
He featured on the weather vane above the old west stand. Legend had it that if the weather vane was removed, Chelsea would suffer. Phooey? When it was taken down during redevelopment, Chelsea fell to Division 2, came close to bankruptcy, almost lost the Bridge to developers and had to sell many of their most promising players.

10. The black and blue shirts

A colour change sanctioned by manager Tommy Docherty, who fell for the stylish black stripes on navy when he saw Inter Milan sporting the colour scheme. The strip was first worn in the spring of 1966 for an FA Cup semi-final against Sheffield Wednesday, but Chelsea were beaten 2-0. The team believed the changed strip was cursed and fought all attempts to reintroduce it for subsequent games.

11. Gary Chivers

Insisted on running out on to the pitch after the captain and the goalie. "I always did it," he said. "I still don't know why, but it always had to be captain, goalie then me."

FIRST AND FOREMOST

11 best league finishes

1. **2004/05** 1st
   1954/55 1st
3. **2003/04** 2nd
4. **1998/99** 3rd
   1969/70 3rd
   1964/65 3rd
   1919/20 3rd
8. **2002/03** 4th
   1997/98 4th
10. **1999/2000** 5th
    1989/90 5th
    1968/69 5th

FIRST AND LAST

11 players who made just one appearance for the Blues

1. **Stanley Macintosh** 1930-36
2. **Murdoch Dickie** 1945-46
3. **Colin Court** 1954-59
4. **Mike Pinner** 1961-62
5. **John O'Rourke** 1963
6. **Roger Wosahlo** 1964-67 as sub

11. FOREIGNERS: THE FIRST LINE-UP OF NON-BRITS IN ENGLAND

Ed de Goey (Holland)

Albert Ferrer (Spain)   Celestine Babayaro (Nigeria)

Emerson Thome (Brazil)   Frank Leboeuf (France)

Didier Deschamps (France)

Roberto Di Matteo (Italy)

Dan Petrescu (Romania)

Gustavo Poyet (Uruguay) capt

Tore Andre Flo (Norway)

Gabriele Ambrosetti (Italy)

The 11 Chelsea players in the first all-foreign English league line-up Southampton v Chelsea, Boxing Day 1999. Chelsea won 2-1.

7. **Alex Stepney** 1966
8. **Kingsley Whiffen** 1966-67
9. **Paul McMillan** 1967-68
10. **Jimmy Clare** 1977-81 as sub
11. **Steve Livingstone** 1993-94 as sub

FORM AN ORDERLY QUEUE

Highest number of Chelsea players to score in a league season

1. **18 players** 2003/04
   18 players 1996/07
   18 players 1909/10
4. **17 players** 1999/2000
   17 players 1945/46
6. **16 players** 2002/03
   16 players 1998/99
   16 players 1997/98

16 players 1991/92
16 players 1986/87
16 players 1974/75
16 players 1928/29
16 players 1927/28

FRENCH FANCIES

The 11 Chelsea players who took part in the 1998 World Cup in France

1. **Graeme Le Saux** England
2. **Ed de Goey** Holland
3. **Celestine Babayaro** Nigeria
4. **Brian Laudrup** Denmark
5. **Roberto Di Matteo** Italy
6. **Albert Ferrer** Spain
7. **Frank Leboeuf** France
8. **Marcel Desailly** France
9. **Dan Petrescu** Romania
10. **Frank Sinclair** Jamaica
11. **Tore Andre Flo** Norway

FREQUENT FLIERS

The 11 players with most appearances for Chelsea in the Champions League

1. **Frank Lampard** 23+1
2. **William Gallas** 23
3. **John Terry** 23
4. **Claude Makelele** 21
5. **Marcel Desailly** 18+1
6. **Damien Duff** 15+6
7. **Eidur Gudjohnsen** 15+4
8. **Celestine Babayaro** 15
9. **Wayne Bridge** 14+2
10. **Ed de Goey** 14
11. **Gianfranco Zola** 14

FROM STUCK IN TO DUG OUT

11 Chelsea players who also managed the club

1. John Tait Robertson player-manager 1905/06
Signed from Glasgow Rangers, he helped the club achieve third place in its first year.
2. Ken Shellito player 1958/9-1965/66, manager 1977-78
Right-back who finished 16th in his first season in charge, and was rapidly replaced.
3. Tommy Docherty player 1961/62, manager 1962-67
Better known as a manager than a player, he won the League Cup while in charge.
4. Eddie McCreadie player 1962/3-1973/74, manager 1975-77
Popular choice as gaffer, as was any member of the 1970 FA Cup-winning side.
5. John Hollins player 1963/64-1974/75 and 1983/84, manager 1985-88
Another who was able to bask in the reflected glory of his on-pitch achievements.
6. David Webb player 1967/68-1973/74, manager 1993
A brief managerial reign to plug the gap between Ian Porterfield and Glenn Hoddle.
7. Glenn Hoddle player/manager 1993-96
Lured from the Bridge by the England job, he helped dig the modern foundations.
8. Ruud Gullit player/manager 1996-98
Cult figure on and off the pitch, his charisma attracted a host of stars to the club.
9. Gianluca Vialli player/manager 1996-2000
Strong, skilled forward who helped fill the trophy cabinet with cups.
10. Ray Wilkins player 1973/74-1978/79 **Graham Rix** player 1994/95 both had
stints as assistant manager in the late 1990s. Midfield maestro Wilkins steadied the
ship when Rix wound up in chokey.
11. Steve Clarke player 1986/87-1997/98, assistant manager 2004-
A cup winner as a player and coach, he built a firm bond with José Mourinho.

GATEWAY TO BRENTFORD?

11 Chelsea players who went west to Griffin Park

1. **William Brawn** (1907-11)
2. **Peter Buchanan** (1936-46)
3. **John Paton** (1946-47)
4. **Eric Parsons** (1950-56)
5. **Ron Greenwood** (1952-55)
6. **John Brooks** (1959-61)
7. **Ron Harris** (1961-80) was player/coach at Brentford.
8. **Tommy Baldwin** (1966-74)
9. **Petar Borota** (1979-82)
10. **Colin Lee** (1980-87)
11. **Keith Jones** (1983-86)

GERRIM OFF!

11 players the Shed turned against

1. Peter Houseman
Nicknamed Mary, he angered the Shed by failing to take part in the pre-match ritual of waving acknowledgement when his name was chanted. Perceived as a remote loner.

2. Chris Sutton
The £10m man never clicked, netting just one league goal in his only season at the Bridge. Any remaining jot of confidence disappeared as even home fans started jeering each touch.

3. Graham Wilkins
Perhaps lacking the finesse and passing skills of his younger brother Ray, Graham was given a rough ride and regularly jeered from the terraces.

4. Eric Parsons
The Rabbit, as he was always known, had to endure several seasons of abuse from the Stamford Bridge faithful in the early 1950s. To his great credit, he never seemed to let it affect him, and eventually won many doubters over.

5. Dave Beasant
Was showered with abuse in September 1992 after Norwich turned a 2-0 deficit at Stamford Bridge into an unlikely victory thanks to a string of woeful goalkeeping blunders in a nightmare game. His confidence evaporated.

6. Graeme Le Saux
Went through a phase of being booed after tearing off his shirt and hurling it down into the mud at the side of the pitch when Ian Porterfield subbed him at Stamford Bridge in 1992.

7. Jody Morris
Once tipped as the club captain to succeed Dennis Wise, midfielder Morris's endless pub and nightclub 'incidents' figured regularly in the tabloids, and led fans to noisily question why he was being paid so handsomely to contribute so little.

8. John Hollins
The manager was sacked in March 1988 after four long months without a league win. The boos from the Shed hastened his exit.

9. Slavisa Jokanovic
Or Slavisa Joke-on-the-pitch, as he was known. Played 28 games for Chelsea, plus 25 appearances as sub, but was booed by fans who simply never rated him. He cost £1.7m from Deportivo La Coruna, but most supporters would have been happy to get £1.70 for the No 10. One ironic chant was: "You've got Di Canio, we've got Jokanovic!"

10. Jerry Murphy
After 39 games (and three goals) between 1985 and 1988, the terraces had had enough of the midfielder and made their feelings clear. Bobby Campbell agreed with the supporters' verdict and dispensed with his services.

11. Doug Rougvie

Arguably Chelsea's most ungainly player of all time, the big defender attracted more laughter from the fans than cheers. He made 100 appearances in the mid-1980s, but exasperated supporters rather than inspired them.

GINGERS

11 Chelsea redheads

1. David Hopkin
2. Derek Saunders
3. James Argue
4. Erland Johnsen
5. Gareth Hall
6. Ray Lewington
7. Jim Docherty
8. Robert Fleck
9. Duncan Shearer
10. Derek Kevan
11. Joe Payne

GOALSCORERS IN THE 2004/05 TITLE-WINNING SEASON

The year we couldn't help but hit the back of the net

1. **Frank Lampard** 13
2. **Eidur Gudjohnsen** 12
3. **Didier Drogba** 10
4. **Joe Cole** 8
5. **Arjen Robben** 7
6. **Damien Duff** 6
7. **Mateja Kezman** 4
   Tiago 4
9. **John Terry** 3
10. **William Gallas** 2
11. **Ricardo Carvalho** 1
    Claude Makelele 1

GOD SQUAD

11 who believe in more than just Chelsea FC

1. Glenn Hoddle
A born-again Christian who also believes in reincarnation and provoked outrage when he said, in an interview in *The Times*, that he thought disabled people were that way because they were paying for sins in a previous life. Would sooner consult a faith healer than the board.

2. Mateja Kezman
Devout is not a strong enough word. When this Orthodox Christian runs onto the pitch he crosses himself more than the Pope. His body boasts several large, colourful tattoos of Christ and he wears a T-shirt of Christ's face under his club shirt.

3. Celestine Babayaro
A practising Catholic who attended church every Sunday.

4. Claudio Ranieri
Behind the chuckles lurks a Roman Catholic who takes his belief very seriously.

5. Bobby Tambling
Became a Jehovah's Witness.

6. Gavin Peacock
Another born-again Christian.

7. Peter Bonetti
A Roman Catholic. He caught everything else, so no surprise about religion.

8. Ruud Gullit
Once stated in an interview:"I believe in God." Confusingly, his ex-wife, Christina Gullit, said of Ruud:"He thinks he is God, and we are all nobodies."

9. Derek Smethurst
Became a Mormon.

10. Damien Duff
When he isn't crossing for team-mates, he's busy crossing himself.

11. José Mourinho
Is a practising Roman Catholic, while owner Roman Abramovich was brought up in the Jewish faith.

GREATEST GOAL-GRABBERS

11 all-time top goalscorers

1. **Bobby Tambling** (1958-69) 202
2. **Kerry Dixon** (1983-92) 193
3. **Roy Bentley** (1947-56) 150
4. **Peter Osgood** (1964-79) 150
5. **Jimmy Greaves** (1957-60) 132
6. **George Mills** (1929-38) 123
7. **George Hilsdon** (1906-11) 107
8. **Barry Bridges** (1958-65) 93
9. **Tommy Baldwin** (1966-74) 92
10. **Jimmy Floyd Hasselbaink** (2000-04) 87
11. **Hughie Gallacher** (1930-34) 81

GREATEST GOALKEEPERS

Chelsea's 11 top performers between the sticks

1. Peter Bonetti 1960-79
His 729 matches in goal for Chelsea (including 210 clean sheets) seems unlikely to be beaten, unless Petr Cech plays into his forties. The Cat actually played around 1,000 games for the club, if friendlies, testimonials and benefit matches are taken into account. He won the League Cup in 1965, FA Cup in 1970 and Cup Winners' Cup in 1971. His finest hour was arguably the 1970 FA Cup replay against Leeds United at Old Trafford. Despite being seriously injured in a collision with Mick Jones, he remained on the field, limping from post to post to deny Leeds. Had he been forced to hobble off, Dave Webb would have had to stand in… and therefore would not have been in the opposite goalmouth to score the winner! Bonetti won only seven England caps, among them the notorious 1970 World Cup quarter-final in Mexico against West Germany when England threw away a two-goal lead to lose 2-3, provoking years of harsh "Bonetti lost the World Cup" chants from rival fans. Incidentally, the unusual surname comes from the fact that his parents were Swiss.

2. Petr Cech 2004-

Signed from Rennes in France for £7m in the summer of 2004, the Czech Republic's No1 stopper was one of the key figures in the 2004/05 season, helping establish Chelsea's best defensive stats of all time. By saving a Paul Dickov penalty at Blackburn in February 2005 he overtook Peter Schmeichel's record for Manchester United of 694 Premiership minutes without conceding a goal. He continued the epic shut-out to 1,024 minutes, when a goal by Norwich City at Carrow Road on 5 March 2005 brought the run to an end, just 39 minutes short of the all-time English record. His ten consecutive clean sheets in the 2004/05 season is an English record in the top flight, and beats Willie Foulke's nine-match run in Chelsea's very first season. It was originally thought Cech would be understudy to Carlo Cudicini, but his stunning form meant he has become an automatic first choice.

3. Carlo Cudicini 1999-

Chelsea's No23, signed as back-up for Ed de Goey from Castel Di Sangro (Italy's smallest town professional football club), kept 24 clean sheets in 40 games in 2003/04 – a record which would guarantee any other keeper a first-team place. But Petr Cech's arrival pushed the likeable Milan-born netminder (who signed for AC Milan at the age of nine) down to second in the pecking order. Chelsea's 2002 player

11. 11 GREAT FA CUP WINNERS FROM 1970

Peter Bonetti

Ron Harris   Eddie McCreadie

John Dempsey   David Webb

Peter Houseman

John Hollins

Tommy Baldwin   Charlie Cooke

Peter Osgood   Ian Hutchinson

Dave Sexton's Chelsea team, which lifted the 1970 FA Cup after a replay at Old Trafford also included sub Marvin Hinton, who replaced Osgood. This line-up started the replay, with Harris switched to right-back and Dave Webb at centre-half

of the year, he is a terrific penalty saver – blocking six of the first dozen he faced for the Blues. One of the all-time bargain buys at £160,000.

4. **William Foulke** 1905-06

Chelsea's first goalkeeper was a 6ft 3in man mountain who wore size 12 boots and vast shorts. He enjoyed his food so much that while he weighed a staggering 22 stone when he arrived in 1905, he had expanded to a walloping 26 stone by the time he was transferred to Bradford City in April 1906. To intimidate visiting players and impress the crowd, Foulke always took to the field alongside Martin Moran, Chelsea's smallest player at the time. The first club captain, Foulke refused to move to London, and commuted to the Bridge from his home in Sheffield. Ignominiously he ended up saving shots at a penny-a-go beach sideshow. Confusingly, he was registered at birth as Foulk, played football as Foulke and was put down on his death certificate in 1916 as Foulkes.

5. **Benjamin Howard Baker** 1921-26

First-choice keeper for five seasons, HB, as he was known, played 92 league games and conceded just 96 goals – one of the best ratios of all Blues keepers. He is the only goalie to have scored for Chelsea. Two minutes from time in a goalless First Division match against Bradford City at the Bridge in November 1921, Chelsea were awarded a penalty. The captain, Jack Harrow, had missed his last two spot-kicks, so HB sprinted the length of the pitch and scored. A wearer of kneepads and polo-neck jumpers when he played, he is one of Chelsea's longest-lived ex-players, dying five months short of his 95th birthday in 1987.

6. **Victor Woodley** 1931-45

Second only to Peter Bonetti in appearances, he turned out 272 times for the Blues in addition to playing 121 wartime games. Chelsea's first ever-present keeper in a season (42 league games and one cup match in 1932/33), he was popularly regarded as Chelsea's player of the 1930s. He gained 19 international caps for England – a club record which stood for more than 20 years until surpassed by Eddie McCreadie in 1969, for Scotland. He played 252 league games for Chelsea, all in Division 1, achieving 60 clean sheets. Perhaps his proudest achievement was saving a penalty in the famous 3-3 draw at Stamford Bridge against Moscow Dynamo just after World War 2, watched by an estimated 100,000 people.

7. **John Phillips** 1970-79

Signed from Aston Villa as cover for Peter Bonetti after regular reserve Tommy Hughes broke his leg, 19-year-old Phillips suddenly found himself centre-stage. The Cat was injured, so in October 1970 the stand-by stood in, at Bloomfield Road against Blackpool. By the interval Phillips had been beaten three times and it looked like a disastrous debut, but Chelsea managed four second-half goals in the final 20 minutes for a shock turnaround. Phillips excelled in the quarter-final and semi-final of the 1971 Cup Winners' Cup campaign when Bonetti was confined to bed with pneumonia, but unluckily missed out on the successful final against Real Madrid when The Cat recovered. Made 149 appearances for Chelsea.

8. Petar Borota 1979-82
The Yugoslav international keeper was a flamboyant eccentric whose antics were loved and dreaded in equal measure by the Stamford Bridge fans. He wore distinctive continental knee-length shorts and made regular upfield sorties, often to the dismay of his colleagues. Signed for £70,000, he kept a clean sheet on his debut against Liverpool and conceded a total of 146 goals in his 114 games.

9. Eddie Niedzwiecki 1983-87
Could have been higher up the list had it not been for a knee injury in March 1986 which effectively ended his playing career. Born in Wales of Polish parents, he was in goal for 136 league games, conceding 155 goals. Neville Southall's dominating presence in the Wales goal meant the brave and agile keeper only got two caps.

10. Reg Matthews 1956-61
Signed for £20,000 – then a record fee for a goalie – from Coventry City. In the 1956/57 season he was in goal for all of Chelsea's 45 games. He played 135 league games and nine FA Cup matches for the Blues, as well as Chelsea's first League Cup match, a 7-1 thrashing of Millwall at the Den, the club's record score in the competition. He won five full England caps, four England Under 23 caps and three England 'B' international caps.

11. Dave Beasant 1989-92
Lurch made a decent start after his £725,000 signing from Newcastle United, but his confidence seeped away when the goals started leaking. Manager Ian Porterfield spared him further jeers from home fans by sending him on loan to Grimsby and Wolves. Eventually he was bumped out by Dmitri Kharine.

HAIR-DON'TS

11 memorable Chelsea barnets – for the wrong reasons

1. **Petar Borota** domed privet hedge
2. **John Dempsey** comb-over haystack
3. **Ian Britton** Marge Simpson-style cottage loaf
4. **Robert Fleck** impression of a moth-eaten toupé
5. **Paul Elliott** heron's nest in a gale
6. **Mick Hazard** unruly springy bath sponge
7. **Ruud Gullit** locks that spawned an entire joke wig industry
8. **Hernan Crespo** horse's mane held in place by an old bootlace
9. **Mario Stanic** wild-man-of-Borneo effect
10. **Mario Melchiot** curtain of locks that appeared to be chasing him
11. **Ricardo Carvalho** Coco the Clown lookalike

HANG ON, HAVEN'T I SEEN YOU AT OLD TRAFFORD?

11 Reds in our bed

1. **Tommy Meehan** (1920-24) also wore red.
2. **Graham Moore** (1961-63) went on to Manchester United.
3. **Tommy Docherty** (1962-67) was United manager from 1972-77.
4. **Alex Stepney** (1966) played one game for Chelsea and was sold to United where he played in goal 433 times.
5. **Dave Sexton** (manager 1967-74) also managed United.
6. **Ray Wilkins** (1973-79) played 160 times for the Reds between 1979 and 1984.
7. **Bryan 'Pop' Robson** (1982-83) later coached at Old Trafford.
8. **Mickey Thomas** (1984-5) also played 90 times for Manchester United.
9. **Mal Donaghy** (1992-94) arrived at Chelsea shortly before his 35th birthday after

playing 89 games in three years for United.

10. Mark Hughes (1995-98) made more than 100 appearances for the Blues, scoring 39 goals, after being controversially sold by Sir Alex Ferguson following Sparky's glittering career with United (1983-95).

11. Juan Sebastian Veron (2003-) cost United more than £28m in 2001, came to Chelsea for a relative knock-down £15m two years later, and was farmed out to Inter after 14 appearances for the Blues.

HAT-TRICK HUMDINGERS

11 hearteners – and harrowers

1. Jimmy Greaves is still Chelsea's hat-trick king with 13.

2. The only other hat-trick heroes who even come close are George Hilsdon (9), Bobby Tambling (8) and Kerry Dixon (8). Peter Osgood notched five.

3. Manchester City have scored more hat-tricks against Chelsea – six to be precise – than any other side.

4. Eidur Gudjohnsen's hat-trick against Blackburn Rovers at the Bridge in October 2004 was his first in professional football, and came a month after his 26th birthday.

5. The Blues' very first hat-trick came in their first home game in September 1905, when Jimmy Windridge was the hero in a 5-1 defeat of Hull City.

6. Chelsea have only conceded two hat-tricks in the same match on one occasion, when Neil Webb and Gary Birtles had to fight over the match ball following Nottingham Forest's 6-2 win at the Bridge on 20 September 1986.

7. The only Chelsea defender to have scored a hat-trick was Dave Webb at Portman Road on Boxing Day 1968, when the Blues beat Ipswich Town 3-1. John Terry netted two away to Charlton Athletic in November 2004.

8. George 'Gatling Gun' Hilsdon scored a double hat-trick when Chelsea beat Worksop 9-1 in the FA Cup first round on 11 January 1908 at the Bridge.

9. In the 1960/61 season, Jimmy Greaves scored six hat-tricks. The previous season he got three.

10. The only Chelsea hat-trick scored at Wembley was David Speedie's in the Full Members' Cup final on 23 March 1986, in the 5-4 defeat of Manchester City.

11. In October 1957, 16-year-old Bobby Tambling (who would become the Blues' top scorer of all time) scored a hat-trick and Barry Bridges a double hat-trick as Chelsea beat Woodfood Youth 14-0 in the first round of the FA Youth Cup.

HERE WE GO AGAIN...

The 11 players with most appearances for Chelsea in all European competitions

1. **Dennis Wise** 37+1
2. **Gianfranco Zola** 35+2
3. **Marcel Desailly** 35+1
4. **Ed de Goey** 35
5. **Frank Leboeuf** 31+1
6. **Frank Lampard** 30+2
7. **John Terry** 30
8. **Celestine Babayaro** 28+3
9. **William Gallas** 28
10. **John Hollins** 27
10. **Ron Harris** 27

DAVE WEBB IS THE ONLY CHELSEA DEFENDER TO SCORE A HAT-TRICK. JOHN TERRY HAS BAGGED A BRACE

HIGH DAYS AND HOLIDAYS

11 significant dates in Chelsea's history

1. 28 April 1877
Stamford Bridge stadium opens as the home of London Athletic Club.

2. 29 September 1904
Brothers H.A. and J.T. Mears take possession of the ground and begin the task of turning it into a football stadium.

3. 14 March 1905
Chelsea is founded in the Rising Sun pub, opposite the Stamford Bridge hotel entrance.

4. 11 September 1905
A Monday, and Chelsea's first competitive home game. The Blues beat Hull City 5-1.

5. 12 October 1935
Club record attendance of 82,905, for the visit of champions Arsenal.

6. 19 March 1957
Chelsea become the first club to use floodlights, for a friendly against Sparta Prague. In the same year Chelsea became the first English club to travel to a league fixture by air, flying to Newcastle.

7. 5 June 1972
Chairman Brian Mears announces redevelopment plans for Stamford Bridge, including the 12,000-seat, three-tier east stand which will almost bankrupt Chelsea.

8. 27 January 1974
Stoke City v Chelsea is the first top-flight domestic game to be played on a Sunday. Chelsea lose 1-0.

9. 2 April 1982
Ken Bates pays a £1 note for Chelsea, as well as taking on £2m in debts.

10. 22 October 1996
Matthew Harding's fatal helicopter crash.

11. 30 April 2005
A 2-0 victory at Bolton Wanderers' Reebok stadium earns the Blues the league title, half a century to the week after Ted Drake achieved the feat.

HIGHEST POINTS TOTALS

Calculated using three points for a win

1. **99 points** 1988/89
2. **95 points** 2004/05
3. **88 points** 1983/84
4. **79 points** 2003/04
5. **75 points** 1998/99
6. **71 points** 1985/86

7. **67 points** 2002/03
8. **66 points** 1984/85
9. **65 points** 1999/2000
10. **64 points** 2001/02
11. **63 points** 1997/98

HIT THE ROAD, JACK

11 Chelsea players who are really motoring

1. William Steer
2. Jon Harley
3. Micky Hazard
4. David Speedie
5. Roy Bentley
6. Harry Ford
7. Jody Morris
8. Arjen Robben
9. George Horn
10. Phil Driver
11. George Hunter

HOME-GROWN HEROES

11 Chelsea players who came up through the ranks

1. John Terry
Professional Footballers' Association Player of the Year 2005 (the first Chelsea player so honoured), the centre-half emerged from the youth team to become captain. Made his first-team debut in October 1998 under Gianluca Vialli.

2. Jimmy Greaves
The 14-year-old hit five for Dagenham Boys while chief scout Jimmy Thompson was watching from the touchline. Thompson was on the Greaves family doorstep with a contract to sign a month before the lad left school. Greavesie's 114 goals in his second year as an apprentice is a Chelsea junior record unlikely to be beaten.

3. Peter Bonetti

Bless you, Mrs B. The family lived in Putney, so mum dropped a line to that nice Mr Drake at the big club up the road telling him how proud she was of her Peter. On the strength of that letter, The Cat was given a trial. Peter signed in July 1958, was in goal when the Blues won the FA Youth Cup in 1960 and was a first-teamer from then on.

4. Peter Osgood

Don't knock letter-writing. Peter's Uncle Bob got out the Basildon Bond and penned a note to Tommy Docherty. The 16-year-old Ossie was given a trial, but subbed after just half an hour by youth manager Dick Foss. Dejected, our hero walked off, only to be handed forms to sign before any of the other scouts present could make a move.

5. Barry Bridges

Made his debut in February 1959 at 17, scoring in a 3-2 win against West Ham. Was squeezed out for two years before getting a fresh chance to prove what he could do. Showed patience when Frank Upton, then Jimmy Mulholland bumped him out of the first team, but eventually formed a great partnership with Bobby Tambling.

> MRS BONETTI WROTE A LETTER TO MR DRAKE TELLING HIM HOW PROUD SHE WAS OF HER SON PETER

6. Ray Wilkins

The first programme of the 1972/73 season announced that the summer's new apprentices included Raymond Wilkins, 15. Butch had begun training with the Blues at the age of ten, on the strength of having gone to the same school as one of Chelsea's existing juniors. A month after his 17th birthday, he made his senior debut.

7. John Hollins

Not the most promising of starts (he was on the losing side in his first three senior appearances as a 17-year-old in the 1963/64 season), but was given the No 4 shirt the following year, and became a key member of Tommy Docherty's side.

8. Ron Harris

Brought into the first team after impressing the Doc by captaining the England youth team which won the Little World Cup in April 1963. The hard-tackling Chopper was 18 at the time, and went on to make 794 appearances for the Blues – a feat which seems unlikely to be bettered.

9. Bert Murray

Ruby was another of the 1958 apprentice intake, starting on the same day as Allan

Harris, Bonetti, Venables and Tambling. Although in and out of the Doc's teams, he was difficult to drop after scoring the goal that forced an FA Cup third round replay against Spurs in 1964, then a goal that helped knock Tottenham out.

10. Bobby Tambling
Began to make regular first-team appearances in the 1960/61 season as a winger and, later, inside-forward. When Jimmy Greaves left for Italy, the mantle fell on Tambling's shoulders. He didn't fail. Still Chelsea's record goalscorer with 202 strikes in 370 games. At 21 he was the youngest captain of a promotion-winning side.

11. Terry Venables
Became a Chelsea player on his 15th birthday, 6 January 1958 – although he actually signed as an amateur because he was hoping to play for England in the 1960 Rome Olympics. When he failed to figure in the Olympic squad, Terry signed professional forms at Stamford Bridge, making him one of Ted Drake's famous Ducklings.

HOWZAT!
11 Chelsea players who were serious cricketers

1. Willie Foulke 1905-6
Played four matches as a professional cricketer for Derbyshire in the summer of 1900. A middle-order batting all-rounder, his highest first-class score was 53 and his best bowling figures 2 for 15.

2. Ben Howard Baker 1921-26
Played for Liverpool Cricket Club in the summer when he wasn't in goal for Chelsea.

3. Joe Payne 1938-46
A striker for Chelsea who played county cricket for Bedfordshire.

4. Leslie Compton occasional full-back for Chelsea during World War 2
Kept wicket for Middlesex. His brother was somewhat better known in the cricketing world – fellow Middlesex player and England international Denis.

5. Len Dolding 1945-48
Made 26 appearances for Chelsea, scoring two goals, and also played cricket for the MCC and Middlesex.

6. Harry Medhurst 1946-52
Chelsea's smallest goalkeeper at 5ft 9in, he also played for Surrey's 2nd XI.

7. Frank Mitchell 1949-52
Played 17 first class matches for Warwickshire County Cricket Club.

8. Peter Pickering 1948-51
Chelsea goalie who played for Northamptonshire (top score 37), and went on to become a first-class cricket umpire in South Africa.

9. Frank Blunstone 1953-64
Played cricket for Cheshire.

10. Ron Tindall 1955-64
Was a regular Surrey all-rounder between 1956 and 1966, and one of their finest catchers. His best bowling figures were 3 for 43. When he left Surrey he emigrated and became director of coaching for the West Australia Cricket Association.

11. Ron Harris 1961-80
Yes, Chopper Harris. The player who has made most appearances for Chelsea also played cricket for England schoolboys.

I'LL HAVE AN 'H' PLEASE, BOB

11 Chelsea greats from the 1960s whose names began with H

1. Allan Harris
2. Ron Harris
3. Mike Harrison
4. Tony Hateley
5. Marvin Hinton
6. John Hollins
7. Peter Houseman
8. Stewart Houston
9. Alan Hudson
10. Tommy Hughes
11. Ian Hutchinson

> RON TINDALL WAS A TOP SURREY CATCHER, AND WENT ON TO BECOME AN AUSSIE CRICKET COACH

IN THEIR OWN WORDS

11 Chelsea players' autobiographies

1. **Dave Beasant** *Tales Of The Unexpected*
2. **Alan Hudson** *The Working Man's Ballet*
3. **Ron Greenwood** *Yours Sincerely*
4. **Ruud Gullit** *My Autobiography*
5. **Jimmy Greaves** *This One's On Me*
6. **Kerry Dixon** *Kerry*
7. **Tommy Lawton** *Football is My Business*
8. **Peter Osgood** *Ossie The Wizard*
9. **Roy Bentley** *Going For Goal*
10. **Peter Bonetti** *Leaping To Fame*

11. Terry Venables *Venables, The Autobiography*

Gullit doesn't pull punches in his version of events, and claims credit for much of the Blues' recent success. Greavsie is always a good read, but the pick is El Tel's tome.

ISN'T THAT...?

11 familiar-looking blokes on the touchline at Loftus Road

1. John Crawford Chelsea, 1923-34
Played for QPR and became their first team coach in 1937.

2. William Birrell Chelsea manager, 1939-52
Was at the QPR helm from 1935-39 before steering Chelsea to two wartime cup finals and two FA Cup semi-finals.

3. Les Allen Chelsea, 1954-59
Went on to manage QPR from December 1968 to January 1971.

4. Ken Shellito Chelsea, 1957-69
Later managed Chelsea and QPR.

5. Terry Venables Chelsea, 1960-66
Played for, and later managed, QPR. He was at Loftus Road as a player from 1969-75 and as manager from 1980-84.

6. Tommy Docherty Chelsea manager 1962-67
Twice managed QPR, in November 1968 and from 1979 to 1980.

7. John Hollins Chelsea, 1963-75 and manager, 1983-84
Was the Hoops' caretaker manager from November to December 1997, and a reserve team coach.

8. Stewart Houston Chelsea,1967-72
Managed QPR 1996-97.

9. Dave Sexton Chelsea manager 1967-74
Occupied the gaffer's room at Loftus Road from 1974-77.

10. Ray Wilkins Chelsea, 1973-79
Managed QPR from 1994-96.

11. Bobby Campbell Chelsea manager 1988-91
Also coached at Loftus Road.

IT ISN'T FAR ALONG THE FULHAM ROAD

11 Chelsea players who were also Cottagers

1. **Joe Bradshaw** (1909-10) came from Fulham and later managed the Whites.
2. **James Bowie** (1944-51) transferred to Fulham.
3. **Roy Bentley** (1948-56) went on to Craven Cottage.
4. **Barry Lloyd** (1966-69) moved to Fulham.
5. **John Dempsey** (1969-78) came from Fulham.
6. **Teddy Maybank** (1974-76) later played for Fulham.
7. **Ray Lewington** (1974-79) played for Fulham and later managed the Whites.
8. **Clive Walker** (1975-84) was also a Fulham player.
9. **Gordon Davies** (1984-85) was signed from Fulham and later went back there.

10. Doug Rougvie (1984-87) later played for Fulham.
11. Jon Harley (1998-2001) went on to play for Fulham.

ITALIAN CONNECTION

11 Chelsea links with the mighty AC

1. Ray Wilkins had a spell with AC Milan.
2. Jimmy Greaves was sold to AC Milan.
3. Winston Bogarde played for AC Milan.
4. AC Milan loaned George Weah to Chelsea for six months.
5. Christian Panucci played for AC Milan.
6. Ruud Gullit was an AC Milan star.
7. Marcel Desailly was another AC Milan favourite before joining Chelsea.
8. Carlo Cudicini was an AC Milan player they wish they'd hung on to.
9. Hernan Crespo went on loan to AC Milan from Chelsea in 2004, and scored the goals that knocked Manchester United out of the Champions League.
10. Chelsea drew the third round of the Inter-Cities Fairs Cup against AC Milan in March 1966 over two legs, but went through on the toss of a coin.
11. When Arjen Robben broke a bone in his left foot during Chelsea's match at Blackburn in February 2005, he was treated by AC Milan's chiropractor, Jean Pierre Meersseman, sent to London at Roman Abramovich's request.

KINGS FOR A DAY

11 players who captained Chelsea just once

1. Jimmy Greaves
2. Tommy Baldwin
3. Alan Birchenall
4. Joe Kirkup
5. Tony Hateley
6. David Webb
7. Frank Upton
8. Stan Crowther
9. Keith Weller
10. John Bumstead
11. Erland Johnsen

KING'S ROAD? YOU'RE HAVING A LAUGH

11 appalling Chelsea kits

1. In 1994, Chelsea chose for their away colours… tangerine and graphite. A kit so bad it almost defies description. It was as if every clashing design imaginable had been cut and pasted on to one shirt to create a pattern like an early TV testcard. What Coors, the sponsor, made of it isn't recorded. Within weeks of its unveiling it was being sold in bargain bins in the club shop. Must be due a perverse revival.

> IT WAS AS IF EVERY CLASHING DESIGN HAD BEEN CUT AND PASTED ON TO ONE SHIRT LIKE AN OLD TV TESTCARD

2. 1990's royal blue shirt with backgammon board triangles, Commodore sponsor's name and logo, CFC badge, Umbro badge and name, complex open-neck collar with prominent white central neck strip and striped collar. Umbro-branded shorts, held up by bold, visible white drawstring. Blue socks with chequered top and yet another Umbro logo. Too much, too much.

3. 1983's two-tone blue in thin horizontal stripes, Le Coq Sportif logo on one side of the front and the CFC rampant lion and twin stars on the other. Round collar, but with a curious V of material below. The shiny shorts had dark vertical stripes. White socks with two pairs of thin blue hoops, as seen on Colin Pates and Joe McLaughlin.

4. The 1981 home kit was wishy-washy blue with thin white vertical stripes. The lion and stars had shifted to the middle of the shirt.

5. Come 1987, the away colour was jade. Jade? Come off it. A crossover multi-coloured collar could do nothing to dispel the embarrassment.

6. The 1990 away kit of red-and-white diamonds. An early full sponsorship kit, with Commodore emblazoned across the chest. Red just doesn't suit Chelsea.

7. 1997 sees the unloved Autoglass-sponsored shirt, sky blue with bizarre white 'sweat patches' under the arms. An unpopular lurch away from royal blue.

8. The 1988 red-and-white horizontal striped shirts. Enough said.

THEY SAY THAT HODDLE'S FOUND GOD. MUST HAVE BEEN A HELL OF A PASS

9. The 1966 black stripes on navy blue (Inter Milan-style) was a strip with huge potential, devised by Tommy Docherty. The fans liked it, but after the first defeat the players regarded it as unlucky and it was only worn a few times before being given to a local Sunday league team.

10. In 1979 canary yellow with green collars in a skin-tight fabric made Chelsea look like Norwich City. Delia's custard springs to mind.

11. In 1996 the hated tangerine and graphite gives way to… sky blue and yellow. Once again, the shirt appears to have been assembled from offcuts of material chosen at random by a colour-blind tailor.

KNOCK, KNOCK...

11 dreadful Chelsea jokes. Apologies in advance

1. What's blue and falls off tables? Chelsea (in the 1980s).

2. What Chelsea player is also a television programme? Dan Pet-Rescue.

3. Knock knock! Who's there? General Lee! General Lee who? General Lee I support Chelsea, but today I'm backing Fulham.

4. Hoddle's found God. Must have been a hell of a pass. Originated by Jasper Carrott.

5. How many Chelsea fans does it take to change a lightbulb? One. He holds the bulb and expects the world to revolve around him.

6. What do you say to a Chelsea fan with a good-looking bird on his arm? Nice tattoo.

7. Chelsea are releasing a new record at the end of the week. *I'm Forever Blowing Doubles.* (Hey, this was the 1980s.)

8. How can you tell ET is a Chelsea fan? Because he looks like one. (Thought to be a Tottenham joke).

9. What would you get if Manure were relegated? 50,000 more Chelsea fans.

10. Someone asked me the other day, "What time do Chelsea kick off?" I told him, "About every ten minutes". (Old music hall gag.)

11. A Chelsea supporter goes to his doctor to find out what's wrong with him. "Your problem is you're fat," says the doctor. "I'd like a second opinion," says the fan. "OK, you're ugly too," replies the doctor. (OK, enough from the Tottenham jokers.)

LIFE AFTER FOOTBALL

11 Chelsea players and what they did next

1. **Tony Hateley** area rep for a brewery
2. **John Dempsey** social worker
3. **David Cliss** truck driver
4. **Micky Droy** electrical wholesaler
5. **Peter Bonetti** postman
6. **Tony Nicholas** DIY shop manager
7. **Mike Harrison** private healthcare salesman
8. **Reg Matthews** tractor assembly line worker
9. **Reg Williams** magazine printer
10. **Clive Walker** auctioneer
11. **Bobby Tambling** sports shop manager

LOCAL LADS MADE GOOD

11 Chelsea players born within the sound of Stamford Bridge

1. Dennis Wise
2. Alan Hudson
3. Eddie Newton
4. Albert Thain
5. Jason Cundy
6. Graham Stuart
7. Paul Hughes
8. Joe Sheerin
9. Ron Tindall

10. Jody Morris
11. Peter Bonetti

LOCATION, LOCATION, LOCATION

11 songs featuring Chelsea

1. **Midnight in Chelsea** Bon Jovi
2. **Chelsea** Counting Crows
3. **(I Don't Want To Go To) Chelsea** Elvis Costello
4. **Chelsea Monday** Marillion
5. **Chelsea Morning** Joni Mitchell
6. **Chelsea Hotel No 2** Leonard Cohen
7. **Chelsea Hotel** Lloyd Cole
8. **Chelsea Walk** Ocean Colour Scene
9. **Chelsea** Mest
10. **Chelsea Girl** Simple Minds
11. **Chelsea Girls** Velvet Underground

LONG-RANGE MISSILES

11 long-throw specialists

1. Ian Hutchinson
His longest throw was measured at 122ft. "I'm double-jointed at both shoulders, so the throw was actually a flick and then a follow-through," he explained. Nicknamed Windmill Arms because of the way his limbs wheeled after release.

2. Vinnie Jones
A couple of quick wipes on the shirt, and Vinnie could unleash an exocet of a throw to allow Dennis Wise or Andy Townsend to set up Clive Allen.

3. Glen Johnson
A short run-up and a long arcing fling. Proved deadly at the Millennium Stadium in Cardiff in February 2005 when Liverpool defender Sami Hyypia failed to deal with the lob and Didier Drogba prodded home to help the Blues to the Carling Cup.

4. Mario Melchiot
The gangly Dutch right-back was invariably brought forward to take the throw if the ball went out in the opposition half.

5. John Hollins
A terrific fling for a little chap. A slow wind-up was followed by a whiplashed release.

6. David Hopkin
One of the best Scottish long-throwers of all time. His powerful mortars regularly peppered opponents' penalty areas in his spell at the Bridge in the early 1990s.

7. Willie Foulke
Not exactly a throw-in specialist, but thought to be the Chelsea goalie with the longest lob. Could hurl well beyond the halfway line in the days when sodden leather footballs weighed the same as ten-pin bowling balls.

8. Sam Weaver
Acknowledged as English football's first long-throw specialist. He made 125 appearances for Chelsea between 1936 and 1945.

9. John Sparrow
Sparrow's arrow was one of the weapons in Chelsea's armoury in the mid-to late-1970s, feeding the likes of Tommy Langley.

10. Ken Monkou
The gangly Dutchman regularly started attacks with a penetrating throw.

11. Neil Clement
The Chelsea trainee with the longest throw, he became West Brom's top throw-in specialist after leaving Stamford Bridge.

LONG STANDING

11 of Chelsea's tallest players

1. **Ed de Goey** 6ft 6in
2. **Petr Cech** 6ft 5in
3. **Micky Droy** 6ft 4in
4. **Jiri Jarosik** 6ft 4in

5. **Dave Beasant** 6ft 4in
6. **Robert Huth** 6ft 3in
7. **Willie Foulke** 6ft 3in
8. **Stan Wicks** 6ft 3in
9. **Ruud Gullit** 6ft 3in
10. **Jakob Kjeldbjerg** 6ft 3in
11. **David Lee** 6ft 3in

LOOK NORTH

Ten Scots who signed for Chelsea... and Paul Elliott

1. **Bobby Evans** was signed from Celtic in 1960

2. **Jim Mulholland** arrived from Morton in 1962

3. **Pat Nevin** came from Clyde in 1983

4. **Steve Clarke** was signed as a defender from St Mirren in 1987

5. **Eamonn Bannon** came from Hearts in 1979

6. **Charlie Cooke** was signed from Dundee in 1966

7. **Paul Elliott** is a Lewisham boy but was signed from Celtic in 1991

8. **Eddie McCreadie** came south from Falkirk side East Stirlingshire in 1962

9. **Joe Fascione** arrived from Kirkintilloch Rob Roy in 1964

10. **Joe McLaughlin** signed from Morton in 1984

11. **Tommy Knox** another from East Stirlingshire in the summer of 1962

SPARROW'S ARROW WAS ONE OF THE WEAPONS IN CHELSEA'S ARMOURY

LOWEST POINTS TOTALS

Calculated using two points for a win

1. **20 points** 1978/79
2. **28 points** 1912/13
   28 points 1961/62
4. **29 points** 1909/10
   29 points 1914/15
6. **32 points** 1923/24
   32 points 1950/51
8. **33 points** 1938/39
   33 points 1974/75
10. **35 points** 1932/33
    35 points 1952/53

LOYAL SERVANTS

11 testimonial tantalisers

1. Peter Houseman and Tommy Meehan
The two Chelsea players who have been awarded posthumous testimonials. Houseman and his wife were killed in a car crash in March 1977 two years after the player had left for Oxford United, but the club held a benefit match (between Chelsea 1970 and Chelsea 1977) for their two children. In harsher times, Meeham (1920-24) had died in hospital at the age of 28.

2. Gianfranco Zola
More than 38,000 people turned up at Stamford Bridge for Zola's tribute match in August 2004. The Blues beat Real Zaragoza 3-0.

3. Graham Rix
Scored in an XI which lost 8-5 to Arsenal in Paul Merson's 1996 testimonial.

4. Ian Hutchinson, Peter Bonetti and Ron Harris
All three had two Chelsea testimonials apiece.

5. Steve Kember
Alec Stewart (England cricketer and lifelong Chelsea fan) scored twice for Chelsea Old Boys in a 2004 warm-up game before Kember's testimonial.

6. Ray Wilkins
Made 160 appearances for Manchester United after leaving Chelsea, but the only time he played at the Bridge in a United shirt was in Peter Bonetti's 1979 testimonial.

7. Celestine Babayaro
His sudden move to Newcastle United in January 2005 denied him the chance of a Chelsea testimonial, so the Magpies paid him an extra lump sum as compensation.

8. Eddie Niedzwiecki
The FA fined David Speedie £700 for dropping his shorts during the keeper's testimonial in 1989.

9. Bobby Tambling
In his testimonial match in 1968 the surprise scorer of two Chelsea penalties was… goalie Peter Bonetti.

10. Augustus Harding
Benefited from one of the earliest Chelsea testimonials (in 1913), despite only playing four matches for the Blues over seven years.

11. George 'Gatling Gun' Hilsdon
Earned £90 from his 1912 testimonial – the equivalent of £6,000 in today's money.

> RAY WILKINS ONLY WORE A UNITED SHIRT AT CHELSEA DURING PETER BONETTI'S TESTIMONIAL GAME

MAP REFERENCES

11 Chelsea players with place names from near and far

1. Chris Sutton
2. Jack Sherborne
3. Joe Walton
4. Frank Lyon
5. Steven Hampshire
6. Colin Hampton
7. Steve Sherwood
8. Michael Pinner
9. Keith Dublin
10. Stewart Houston
11. Alex Stepney

MEN OF HARLECH

11 Chelsea players who played for Wales

1. **Mark Hughes** 72 caps
2. **Joey Jones** 72 caps
3. **Peter Nicholas** 58 caps
4. **Micky Thomas** 51 caps
5. **Graham Moore** 21 caps
6. **Gordon Davies** 18 caps
7. **Billy Hughes** 10 caps
8. **Tom Hewitt** 8 caps
9. **Evan Jones** 7 caps

10. John Phillips 4 caps
11. Eddie Niedzwieki 2 caps

MISFIRING MISFITS

11 strikers who never struck in league outings

1. Robert Fleck 40 games, 3 goals
Kept trying, but the talent, flair and cavalier style that delighted crowds at Norwich only flickered, and the fans began to get on his back. The Scottish international, signed for £2.1m in 1992, was sold back to Norwich for £650,000 in 1995. "The supporters were great, but I was glad to get away. It was a hell-hole" Fleck confessed.

2. Chris Sutton 28 games, 1 goal
Was rapidly dubbed Miss Sutton. Chelsea paid Blackburn Rovers £10m in the summer of 1979 after Luca Vialli enthused about the striker's performances against the Blues. He missed two open goals on his debut against Sunderland, and never really recovered. Dropped back to centre-back but was sold on for £6m after getting as many red cards as he did league goals.

3. Gordon Davies 13 games, 6 goals
It looked so good for Ivor, as he was nicknamed. He scored on his debut after signing from Fulham in 1984, got a hat-trick a fortnight later, but then just two in the next 11 games as his game and his prospects seemed to fall apart.

> CHELSEA PAID BLACKBURN £10M FOR CHRIS SUTTON. BUT HE WAS RAPIDLY DUBBED 'MISS' SUTTON

4. Tony Hateley 27 games, 6 goals
With 68 goals in 127 appearances for Villa, the £100,000 record fee seemed money well spent by Tommy Docherty after young Peter Osgood broke his leg in October 1966. But the lurching, ponderous Hateley failed to maintain that ratio and at the end of the season, when Ossie was fit again, he was flogged to Liverpool.

5. Duncan McKenzie 15 games, 4 goals
The 28-year-old striker had a good history of scoring at Leeds United and Everton, but seemed incapable of doing the business at Stamford Bridge. It had been hoped that the £165,000 signing would reproduce his Goodison Park form, but after a measly return in four months of the 1978/79 season, he was resold at half price to Blackburn Rovers.

6. David Mitchell 7 games, 0 goals

The Glasgow-born striker had, rather impressively, won international caps for Australia and played for Feyenoord and Eintracht Frankfurt. He arrived at Chelsea in 1988, and spent three less than happy years at the club. Aggressive and strong he may have been, but the stats told their own story. He made only seven appearances, scored precisely zero goals and vanished on loan to Newcastle.

7. Alexander MacFarland 4 games, 0 goals

An inside-forward, he came south of the border to play for Chelsea in 1913, as the storm clouds of war were gathering. Maybe it was something to do with the London air, but Alex only seemed capable of scoring in Scotland. His miserable statistics look even worse because they were spread over three years. He had better luck with his career in management, at Charlton, Dundee and Blackpool.

8. Steve Livingstone 1 game, 0 goals

He arrived from Blackburn in 1993 as part of a player exchange which saw Graeme Le Saux travel north. What a rotten bit of business. The clunky, clumsy striker made one appearance, and was then dispatched to Grimsby. It eventually cost Chelsea a small fortune to buy Le Saux back. It could be said the 2004/05 season might have been better still had Mateja Kezman been sent to Grimsby...

9. Trevor Aylott 29 games, 2 goals

It all looked so good in October 1977 when Chelsea, who had failed to score in four games, signed the strong 19-year-old. Aylott's debut goal cemented a Chelsea win, and he scored again in his second game to earn another victory. But that was it. For the next 30 matches he failed to trouble opposing keepers, and he was sold to Barnsley... where he went on to score 26 goals.

10. Adrian Mutu 27 games, 6 goals

"Chim-chiminey, Chim-chiminey, Chim Chim Cheroo, You've got Wayne Rooney but we've got Mutu…" That was the chant that rang out at Goodison Park as the Blues beat Everton 1-0 in November 2003. Make that "You've lost Wayne Rooney and we've lost Mutu." He scored on his debut and bagged a further three more in the next two games – a rate not to be sniffed at. Alas, sniffing may have proved his downfall. A seven-month world ban was the punishment for a positive cocaine test, leaving Chelsea's lawyers to see if any of his £15.8m fee to Parma could be recovered.

11. John Brooks 46 games, 6 goals

By no means the worst stats for a Chelsea forward, but it isn't a great hit rate for an

England international striker, especially one who had already performed well when he played for Spurs. Johnny boy stayed at Stamford Bridge from 1959 until 1961, and was sold to Brentford. Nuff said.

MISTAKES, WE'VE MADE A FEW

11 players Chelsea should have hung on to

1. Jimmy Greaves
Sold to AC Milan in 1961. Greaves captained the Blues for his last match, at home to Nottingham Forest, and scored all four goals in the 4-3 win. The following year he returned from Italy, to join London rivals Spurs where he continued his free-scoring career.

2. Gianfranco Zola
Roman Abramovich arrived two weeks too late. Chelsea, struggling under a mountain of debt, asked the mighty midget to take a 40 per cent pay cut. He opted to return to Cagliari. A man of honour, he stuck to his agreement with the Sardinians even when Chelsea improved the offer in the light of the rosier financial situation.

3. Charlie Cooke
The Scottish international winger was sold to Crystal Palace in September 1972, but had to be bought back two years later.

4. Keith Weller
Sold to Leicester City. Dave Sexton later admitted: "Selling Weller was the biggest mistake I ever made."

5. Peter Osgood
Was transfer-listed after a training ground bust-up with Dave Sexton in 1974, eventually moving to Southampton for £275,000.

6. Alan Hudson
Sold to Stoke City in 1974 for £240,000, helping the Potters rise from the bottom five to finish in the top five.

7. David Speedie
Was sold by John Hollins, just before the manager himself was sacked. Hollins later admitted he had been wrong.

8. Ray Wilkins

Sold to Manchester United in August 1979 for £825,000, arguably when the club (just demoted) needed him most. Blues manager Danny Blanchflower had already stripped Butch of the captain's armband, and Dave Sexton pounced to take him to Old Trafford. There he made 160 appearances before moving to AC Milan.

9. Alex Stepney

Played once in goal for Chelsea, but went on to make more than 500 appearances for Manchester United, including winning the European Cup in 1968. Mind you, he'd have had to settle for being Bonetti's cover.

10. Barry Bridges

Moved to Birmingham City in May 1966 for £55,000, after falling out with manager Tommy Docherty. Continued scoring freely after further moves to QPR and Millwall.

11. Dario Gradi

Denied the chance to manage Chelsea, the promising assistant (he understudied Dave Sexton from 1971-74) went on to enjoy a long and widely admired career at Crewe Alexandra, proving his ability to develop young talent and inspire mediocre players to undreamed-of heights. What could he have done with the curious odds-and-sods mixture of Blues in the 1980s? Sadly, we never discovered.

MOST CLEAN SHEETS IN A LEAGUE SEASON

And the first-choice keepers who helped keep them that way

1. **25** Petr Cech, 2004/05
2. **21** Carlo Cudicini, 2003/04
3. **20** Robert Whiting, 1906/07
4. **19** Peter McKenna, 1925/26
   19 Peter Bonetti, 1964/65
6. **18** James Molyneux, 1910/11
   18 James Molyneux, 1919/20
   18 Ben Howard Baker, 1921/22
   18 Ben Howard Baker, 1924/25
   18 Simeon 'Sam' Millington, 1926/27
   18 Petar Borota, 1980/81

MOST LEAGUE GOALS CONCEDED

The 11 seasons when jokes about colanders were most plentiful

1. **1960/61** 100 goals
2. **1958/59** 98 goals
3. **1961/62** 94 goals
4. **1978/79** 92 goals
5. **1959/60** 91 goals
6. **1946/47** 84 goals
7. **1934/35** 82 goals
8. **1938/39** 80 goals
9. **1957/58** 79 goals
10. **1955/56** 77 goals
11. **1912/13** 73 goals
    1931/32 73 goals
    1932/33 73 goals
    1956/57 73 goals

MOST LEAGUE GOALS SCORED

That's more like it! The 11 seasons when most onions were bagged

1. **1960/61** 98 goals
2. **1988/89** 96 goals
3. **1905/06** 90 goals
4. **1964/65** 89 goals
5. **1957/58** 83 goals
6. **1954/55** 81 goals
    1962/63 81 goals
8. **1906/07** 80 goals
    1983/84 80 goals
10. **1958/59** 77 goals
11. **1925/26** 76 goals
    1959/60 76 goals

MOST SUCCESSFUL MANAGERS OVER THEIR FIRST 100 GAMES

Percentage success rate using two points for a win and one for a draw

Manager	P	W	D	L	F	A	%
1. Gianluca Vialli	100	54	26	20	155	80	67.0
2. Claudio Ranieri	100	50	27	23	183	107	63.5
3. Bobby Campbell	100	48	31	21	186	140	63.5
4. Dave Sexton	100	47	27	26	157	124	60.6
5. John Hollins	100	43	26	31	139	139	56.0
6. Tommy Docherty	100	40	20	40	169	154	50.0
7. Glenn Hoddle	100	34	31	35	119	119	49.5
8. Ted Drake	100	33	31	36	151	153	48.5
9. John Neal	100	33	31	36	134	139	48.5
10. Leslie Knighton	100	36	21	43	164	176	46.5
11. David Calderhead	100	36	20	44	146	166	46.0

NATURE BOYS

11 players' names that occur in the wild

1. George Stone
2. David Webb
3. Paul Berry
4. Robert Bush
5. Chris Garland
6. Robert Warren
7. Darren Wood
8. David Hay
9. George Lake
10. Danny Blanchflower
11. Dennis Sorrell

NOTHING ELSE TO DO?

11 embarrassingly low Chelsea gates

1. **3,000** Chelsea v Lincoln City, League, 17 February 1906
2. **3,000** Crystal Palace v Chelsea, FA Cup, 18 November 1905
3. **3,714** Charlton Athletic v Chelsea, Full Members' Cup, 23 October 1985
4. **3,935** Wrexham v Chelsea, League, 27 February 1982
5. **4,000** Wiener SC v Chelsea, Inter-Cities Fairs Cup, 17 November 1965
6. **4,579** Tranmere Rovers v Chelsea, League Cup, 28 October 1982
7. **4,767** Chelsea v Plymouth, Full Members' Cup, 9 November 1988
8. **5,000** Chelsea v 1st Grenadiers, FA Cup, 7 October 1905
9. **5,630** Chelsea v Workington, League Cup, 24 October 1960
10. **6,009** Chelsea v Leyton Orient, League, 5 May 1982
11. **6,677** Chelsea v Carlisle, League, 12 March 1983

NOW THAT'S WHAT I CALL AN AWAY GAME

11 odd locations for Chelsea matches

1. Baghdad 1986
During the Iran-Iraq war in a pre-season friendly. Kick-off was delayed for an hour on rumours Saddam Hussein was on his way. He didn't turn up, and Chelsea drew 1-1.

2. Mozambique 1969
Chelsea's games were a welcome distraction for locals in a bloody civil war. There were tanks on the streets. Chelsea won 9-3 and 2-1. One opponent was barefoot.

3. Tehran 1973
Chelsea visited Iran for three matches, diplomatically losing 1-0 to the national side.

4. Tromso 1997
Cup Winners' Cup game 210 miles inside the Arctic Circle, in blizzard conditions. From time to time the ball was only visible because it was bright orange.

5. Malta 1963
Though a pre-season friendly, sub Tommy Docherty decked a Maltese player.

6. Haiti 1964
The match against the national team was abandoned in hurricane-force winds.

7. El Salvador 1971
Shots were fired outside the team hotel ahead of a couple of matches in the banana republic, on a tour that followed the Blues' Cup Winners' Cup triumph in Greece.

8. Uruguay 1929
Chelsea were one of the first British teams to tour South America – the club's epic expedition in May and June also included Argentina and Brazil.

9. Barbados 1972
A sunny summer tour and a friendly game, which finished Chelsea 10, Barbados 0.

10. Algeria 1951
Bobby Smith scored six goals in four matches during a jaunt to North Africa.

11. Tasmania 1965
Chelsea played 11 games in Oz, beating Tasmania 12-0.

ONE-CAP WONDERS

The wonder is that they didn't get more

1. Ken Shellito
2. John Hollins
3. Ken Armstrong
4. Ben Howard Baker
5. William Brown
6. Jackie Crawford
7. Willie Foulke
8. Harold Halse
9. Percy Humphreys
10. Tommy Meehan
11. Joe Payne

"ONE KINGSLEY WHIFFEN…"

11 monikers to marvel at

1. Les Fridge
2. Perry Digweed
3. Tommy Ord
4. Kingsley Whiffen
5. Mickey Nutton
6. Jack Cock
7. Jimmy Argue
8. Joe Kirkup
9. John Sitton
10. Mike Brolly
11. Ralph Oelofse

PAINTER'S PALETTE
11 Chelsea players with colourful names

1. Seth Plum
2. Alex White
3. William Brown
4. Billy Gray
5. Ron Greenwood
6. Bjarne Goldbaek
7. John Brown
8. John Browning
9. John Dunn
10. Norman Fairgray
11. Ben Whitehouse

PENALTY POINTS
11 teasers that hit the spot

1. Willie Foulke
Saved the first penalty in Chelsea's first game (Stockport, 1905). Chelsea still lost, 1-0.

2. Tommy Lawton
In 1936 the Chelsea forward (playing for Scotland at Wembley) had to place the ball on the spot three times, only to watch it roll away each time because of the high winds. When the gusts briefly died down, he stepped forward calmly and scored.

THE PERFECT 11 FROM THE SOARAWAY SIDE OF 2005

Petr Cech

Paulo Ferreira

William Gallas

Ricardo Carvalho   John Terry

Claude Makelele

Frank Lampard

Joe Cole

Damien Duff

Arjen Robben

Didier Drogba

The usual 2004/05 line up.
Substitutes: Carlo Cudicini,
Robert Huth, Tiago, Alexey
Smertin, Eidur Gudjohnsen.
Manager: José Mourinho

3. Kevin Hitchcock
Made his first penalty save for Chelsea in a league game at Wimbledon's Plough Lane ground in 1988… denying his future Chelsea captain Dennis Wise.

4. Mateja Kezman
The striker's first goal for Chelsea finally arrived in his 13th game for the club – a penalty in the Carling Cup match against West Ham at the end of October 2004.

5. Bob McRoberts
The first player to score a penalty for Chelsea was the moustachioed centre-half, against Barnsley, on 4 November 1905.

6. Graham Roberts
Set a club record by scoring 13 penalties for Chelsea in the 1988/89 season.

7. Dmitri Kharine
Saved three successive penalties in 1994, all away from home, against Newcastle United, Viktoria Zizkov and Sheffield Wednesday.

8. Kevin Hitchcock

Triumphed in every penalty shoot-out competition for Chelsea: against Ipswich at home in the Zenith Data Systems Cup in 1991, against Ajax in the Makita tournament at White Hart Lane in 1993, against Newcastle United away in the 1996 FA Cup, and against Blackburn Rovers at home in the 1997 Coca-Cola Cup.

9. Johnny Bumstead

Once took a spot kick for Chelsea in a match against Watford, and missed. However, the referee had spotted an infringement, and ordered the kick to be retaken. He missed again.

10. Ben Howard Baker

The only Chelsea keeper to score for the club. He took a penalty in November 1921 as the Blues beat Bradford City 1-0 at Stamford Bridge.

11. Pat Nevin

Realising that the Manchester City keeper wasn't paying attention after Chelsea had been awarded a penalty in the Milk Cup in November 1984, Nevin dispensed with a run-up and took the spot kick quickly. Unfortunately it stuck in the mud as it rolled towards goal, and didn't even reach the goal line. "That is without doubt the worst penalty I've ever seen", commented Barry Davies.

PLAYER SWAPS

I'll give you one Wayne Bridge for two Graeme Le Sauxs

1. **Tommy Boyd** (1991-92) for Celtic's Tony Cascarino
2. **Les Allen** (1954-59) for Spurs' Johnny Brooks
3. **Joe Payne** (1938-46) for West Ham keeper Harry Medhurst
4. **George Graham** (1964-66) for Arsenal forward Tommy Baldwin
5. **Ron Tindall** (1955-61) for West Ham's Andy Malcolm
6. **Graeme Le Saux** (1987-93) for Blackburn Rovers' Steve Livingstone
7. **Joe Kirkup** (1966-68) for Southampton's David Webb
8. **Cliff Huxford** (1955-59) was exchanged for Southampton's Charlie Livesey
9. **Tony McAndrew** (1982-84) was swapped for Middlesbrough's Darren Wood
10. **Graeme Le Saux** (1997-2003) crossed on the M3 with Saints' Wayne Bridge
11. **Adrian Mutu** (2003-04) was exchanged for fresh air

PLAYERS OF THE YEAR (1)

The first 11 winners of the Chelsea Supporters Club award, decided by members

1. **Micky Droy** 1978
2. **Tommy Langley** 1979
3. **Clive Walker** 1980
4. **Petar Borota** 1981
5. **Mike Fillery** 1982
6. **Joey Jones** 1983
7. **Pat Nevin** 1984
8. **David Speedie** 1985
9. **Eddie Niedzwiecki** 1986
10. **Pat Nevin** 1987
11. **Tony Dorigo** 1988

PLAYERS OF THE YEAR (2)

The first 11 winners of Chelsea FC's annual award, decided by poll of all fans

1. **Peter Bonetti** 1967
2. **Charlie Cooke** 1968
3. **David Webb** 1969
4. **John Hollins** 1970
5. **John Hollins** 1971
6. **David Webb** 1972
7. **Peter Osgood** 1973
8. **Gary Locke** 1974
9. **Charlie Cooke** 1975
10. **Ray Wilkins** 1976
11. **Ray Wilkins** 1977

QUICK WITS

11 one-off Chelsea chants

1. "We're going to take the Iranian Embassy!"
Chanted in May 1980 while the famous siege was going on just down the road.

2. "Is that all, is that all, is that all she gets at home?"
Sung when a male streaker ran across the pitch during the FA Cup game against Shrewsbury, January 2002.

3. "Sing when you're fishing, you only sing when you're fishing"
To Hull City fans in the FA Cup, December 1999. Other versions include "Sing when you're shearing" (to Derby County fans) and "Sing when you're rowing" (to Oxford United fans).

4. "Woodcock, Woodcock, show us your cock!"
To Arsenal's Tony Woodcock when he took corners in front of the Shed. To the player's credit, he responded by briefly whipping down his shorts.

5. "You're shish, and you know you are!"
To visiting Galatasaray fans. Marvellous.

6. "Ou est Cantona? Said ou est Cantona?"
Urban sophistication reached a new peak with this clever jibe when Leeds United came to the Bridge after Eric Cantona's sale to Manchester United.

7. "Sing when it's snowing, you only sing when it's snowing" – rapidly followed by "What's it like to play on grass?"
Tromso supporters were given plenty of ribbing at Stamford Bridge after the farcical snow-bound first leg of the Cup Winners' Cup match in Norway.

8. "Down like a soufflé, you're going down like a soufflé"
A jibe at Delia Smith as Chelsea beat Norwich 3-1 at Carrow Road in March 2005.

9. "One Harvey Nichols, there's only one Harvey Nichols!"
To Fulham fans whose chairman Mohamed Al Fayed owns Harrods.

10. "One Mrs Parlour, there's only one Mrs Parlour!" and "She's f**king loaded!"
Aimed at Ray Parlour after the divorce lawyers took him to the cleaners.

11. "Normal service has resumed"
Sung at Tottenham (to the tune of: Guide me, Oh Thou Great Redeemer*) after Chelsea continued their undefeated run at 'Three Point Lane' following a rare League Cup blip.*

QUOTE, UNQUOTE

11 memorable sayings from Stamford Bridge

1. "I thought that coming to Chelsea was the best idea I'd ever had. That is until I saw Stamford Bridge. It was a terrible mess and a real shock. I thought to myself: Jesus Christ, what did I do?" **Ruud Gullit**

2. "That'll be the price of a good left-back in 20 years' time." **Ken Bates**, when he was negotiating to borrow £16.5m from the Royal Bank of Scotland in 1992.

3. "I wish I could have taken Alan Hudson with me to Manchester United, to captain that terrific young side there." **Tommy Docherty**

4. "When I look at John Terry and see his fantastic commitment, I can't do anything else but follow him and die on the pitch for him." **Petr Cech**

> I GET THE BEST FROM MY PLAYERS WHEN THE FISH IS DOWN... ER, CHIPS

5. "I don't want to be the club cretin." **Frank Leboeuf**

6. "I get the best from my players when the fish is down." **Gianluca Vialli** *(Asked by baffled reporters to clarify the remark, he altered it to "chips")*

7. "He always carries a large English/Italian phrasebook – not because his English isn't any good, but to stand on." **Graeme Le Saux** on Gianfranco Zola

8. "In those days there was a dog track at Stamford Bridge, and plenty of room behind the goals, so we used to train at the back with the dogs. The dogs used to beat us, that was the trouble." **Jimmy Greaves**

9. "He's the fastest thing on two feet – quick enough to catch pigeons." **George Graham** of teammate Barry Bridges

10. "I have always felt with Ken Bates that he believes in one man, one vote... and he is the one man." **David Mellor**

11. "Chelsea are boring." **Johann Cruyff** *(The remark in 2005 from Barcelona's elder statesman prompted ironic "Boring, boring Chelsea" chants from the Blues faithful).*

REAL HEROES

11 Chelsea players who served their country in wartime

1. Robert Whiting 1906-07
Joined up at the outbreak of World War 1, aged 31, as a private in the Middlesex Regiment. Killed in action in France on 28 April 1917. In his playing days for Chelsea, as a goalkeeper with a prodigious kick, he had been nicknamed Pom-Pom after a quick-firing naval anti-aircraft gun.

2. George Hilsdon 1906-12
George earned his 'Gatling Gun' tag well before World War 1, because of his continuous shots on goal. With a nickname like that, there was no avoiding the call-up. He served with the East Surreys, although in early years he was kept away from the front because his brigadier valued his contribution to the regimental teams. In 1918 he was sent to the front and was badly affected by mustard gas in the trenches at Arras. He never played football again.

3. Colin Hampton 1914-23
Served in World War 1 as a machine gunner in Mesopotamia. His car was blown up by Turkish shells and he was taken prisoner and sent on an arduous route-march to Istanbul (or Constantinople as it then was). However, the Armistice was declared just in time, and he diverted to Britain to resume his footballing career after a five-year gap. He was awarded the Military Medal for gallantry.

4. Jack Cock 1919-23
Played the odd wartime game for Brentford and Croydon Common whenever he was home on leave from the army in World War 1. Another player who was awarded the Military Medal.

5. Andy Wilson 1923-31
A centre-forward who had a successful footballing career after World War 1, despite sustaining a serious wound to his left arm during active service.

6. Hughie Gallacher 1930-36
Worked in a munitions factory in Glasgow during World War 1, and was an ARP warden and ambulance driver in Newcastle during World War 2.

7. Tommy Lawton 1936-47
Served in a Footballers' Battalion in World War 2. An offshoot of the Army Physical Training Corps, it played a series of charity matches to raise money for the Red Cross. He rose to the rank of sergeant major.

8. Danny Winter 1946-51
Was a World War 2 bombardier with the Lancashire Territorial Regiment. He fought in France and was evacuated from Dunkirk.

9. Harry Medhurst 1946-52
A World War 2 infantryman who rose to the rank of sergeant.

10. Johnny McNichol 1948-58
Served in the Fleet Air Arm during World War 2, and was mainly based in Scotland.

11. Roy Bentley 1948-56
Served in the Royal Navy during the World War 2, on the destroyers escorting the Atlantic convoys.

SAFE PAIRS OF HANDS

11 international goalkeepers in a Chelsea shirt

1. **Peter Bonetti** England
2. **Vic Woodley** England
3. **Dave Beasant** England
4. **Ben Howard Baker** England
5. **Willie Foulke** England
6. **Johnny Jackson** Scotland
7. **John Phillips** Wales
8. **Eddie Niedzwiecki** Wales
9. **Gerry Peyton** Republic of Ireland
10. **Dmitri Kharine** Russia
11. **Petr Cech** Czech Republic

SCRAMBLED LEGS

11 Chelsea players who would earn top Scrabble scores

1. **Jimmy Floyd Hasselbaink** 51 points
2. **Jakob Kjeldbjerg** 50 points
3. **Boudewijn Zenden** 38 points
4. **Eddie Niedzwiecki** 37 points
5. **Mateja Kezman** 36 points
   Jesper Gronkjaer 36 points
7. **Alexander MacFarland** 35 points
   Micky Hazard 35 points
   Kingsley Whiffen 35 points

Slavisa Jokanovic 35 points
11. Duncan McKenzie 34 points

An honorable mention for **Muzzy Izzet**, who would have scored 49 had he
not been sold before making a first-team appearance. Reserve keeper **Yves
Ma-Kalambay** looks good at a glance, but comes in at a disappointing 33 points.

SECOND-FAVOURITE LEAGUE TABLE

Premiership table, 2004/5

	P	W	D	L	F	A	W	D	L	F	A	Pts
1. Chelsea	38	14	5	0	35	6	15	3	1	37	9	95
2. Arsenal	38	13	5	1	54	19	12	3	4	33	51	83
3. Manchester Utd	38	12	6	1	31	12	10	5	4	27	14	77
4. Everton	38	12	2	5	24	15	6	5	8	21	31	61
5. Liverpool	38	12	4	3	31	15	5	3	11	21	26	58
6. Bolton	38	9	5	5	25	18	7	5	7	24	26	58
7. Middlesbrough	38	9	6	4	29	19	5	7	7	24	27	55
8. Manchester City	38	8	6	5	24	14	5	7	7	23	25	52
9. Tottenham Hotspur	38	9	5	5	36	22	5	5	9	11	19	52
10. Aston Villa	38	8	6	5	26	17	4	5	10	19	35	47
11. Charlton	38	8	4	7	29	29	4	6	9	13	29	46
12. Birmingham	38	8	6	5	24	15	3	6	10	16	31	45
13. Fulham	38	8	4	7	29	26	4	4	11	23	34	44
14. Newcastle United	38	7	7	5	25	25	3	7	9	22	32	44
15. Blackburn	38	5	8	6	21	22	4	7	8	11	21	42
16. Portsmouth	38	8	4	7	30	26	2	5	12	13	33	39
17. West Bromwich Albion	38	5	8	6	17	24	1	8	10	19	37	34
18. Crystal Palace	38	6	5	8	21	19	1	7	11	20	43	33
19. Norwich	38	7	5	7	29	32	0	7	12	13	45	33
20. Southampton	38	5	9	5	30	30	1	5	13	15	36	32

SHALL WE SING A SONG FOR YOU?

11 chants reserved for particular rivals

1. Tottenham Hotspur
(To the tune: *Battle Hymn of the Republic*)

The famous Tottenham Hotspur went to Rome to see the Pope,
The famous Tottenham Hotspur went to Rome to see the Pope,
The famous Tottenham Hotspur went to Rome to see the Pope,
And this is what he said
F**k off!

Who's that team they call the Chelsea?
Who's that team we all adore?
They're the boys in blue and white
And we fight with all our might
And we're out to show the world that we can score.

Barcelona, Real Madrid, Tottenham are a load of Yids
And we're out to show the world that we can score

2. Manchester United
(To the tune: *Glory Glory Hallelujah*)

Who the f**k are Man United?
Who the f**k are Man United?
Who the f**k are Man United?
As the Blues go marching
On, on, on

3. Liverpool and Everton
(To the tune: *The Spinners' In My Liverpool Home*)

In your Liverpool slums
In your Liverpool slums
You look in the gutter for something to eat
You find a dead cat and you think it's a treat
In your Liverpool slums…

4. Manchester United
(To the tune: *Go West*)

Stand up if you hate Man U
Stand up if you hate Man U
Stand up if you hate Man U
Stand up if you hate Man U

5. West Ham United
(To the tune: *Chim Chimminy*, from *Mary Poppins*)

Chim chimminy
Chim chimminy
Chim chim cheroo
We hate those bastards in claret and blue

6. Any vaguely rural teams
(To the tune: *Go West*)

No noise from the tractor boys
No noise from the tractor boys
No noise from the tractor boys
No noise from the tractor boys

7. West Ham United
(To the tune: *I'm Forever Blowing Bubbles*)

I'm forever blowing bubbles
Pretty bubbles in the air
They fly so high
They reach the sky
And like West Ham they fade and die
Tottenham always running
Arsenal running too
We're the Chelsea boot boys, running after you,
Chelsea! Chelsea! Chelsea!

8. Manchester United
60,000 muppets!

9. Liverpool
(To the tune: *You'll Never Walk Alone*)

Sign on, sign on, with pen in your hand
And you'll never get a job
You'll never get a job
Sign on, sign on…

10. Liverpool and Everton
(To the tune: *La Donna e Mobile*)

You nicked my stereo
You nicked my stereo
You nicked my stereo
You nicked my stereo

11. Tottenham Hotspur
(To the tune: *Guide Me, Oh Thou Great Redeemer*)

Does the rabbi
Does the rabbi
Does the rabbi know you're 'ere?

SHORT LIST

11 of Chelsea's littlest big men

1. **Jackie Crawford** (1923-34) 5ft 3in
2. **Martin Moran** (1905-08) 5ft 4in
3. **Norman Fairgray** (1907-14) 5ft 4in
4. **Tommy Miller** (1905-09) 5ft 5in
5. **George Key** (1905-09) 5ft 5in
6. **Tommy Meehan** (1920-24) 5ft 5in
7. **Hughie Gallacher** (1930-34) 5ft 5in
8. **Dick Spence** (1934-47) 5ft 5in
9. **Ian Britton** (1971-82) 5ft 5in
10. **Jody Morris** (1995-2003) 5ft 5in
11. **Gianfranco Zola** (1996-2003) 5ft 5in

SING YOUR HEART OUT FOR THE LADS

11 chants for particular players

1. Albert Ferrer
(To the tune: *Rupert the Bear*)

Albert, Albert Ferrer
Everyone knows his name!

2. Gianfranco Zola
(To the tune: *Can't Take My Eyes Off You*)

Gianfranco Zola, la la la la la la
Gianfranco Zola, la la la la la la
Gianfranco Zola, la la la la la la

3. Peter Osgood
(To the tune: *The First Noel*)

Out from the Shed
Came a rising young star
Scoring goals past Pat Jennings from near and from far
And Chelsea won
As we all knew they would
And the star of that team was Peter Osgood
Osgood, Osgood, Osgood, Osgood
Born is the king of Stamford Bridge

4. Gianluca Vialli
(To the tune: *That's Amore* by Dean Martin)

When the ball hits the net
Like a f**king rocket...
It's Vialli!

5. Ed de Goey
(To the tune: Gary Glitter's *Rock and Roll Part 2*)

Ed de Goey Hey-ey! Ed de Goey
Ed de Goey Hey-ey! Ed de Goey

6. Dennis Wise
(To the tune: *Speedy Gonzales*)

Oh Dennis Wise
Scored a f**king great goal
In the San Siro
Ten minutes to go

7. Frank Lampard
(To the tune: *Skip to My Lou*)

Frank, Frank, super Frank
Frank, Frank, super Frank
Frank, Frank, super Frank, super Frankie Lampard

8. Charlie Cooke (also Frank Leboeuf, Joey Cole and many others)
(To the tune: *The Quartermaster's Stores*)

He's here, he's there
He's every f**king where
Charlie Cooke

9. Dimitri Kharine
(To the tune: *Hava Nagila*)

Kharine, Dimitri Kharine, Dimitri Kharine,
Dimitri Khar-ar-ine, Oi!

10. Tore Andre Flo
(To the tune: *Go West*)

Tore, Tore Andre Flo
Tore, Tore Andre Flo
Tore, Tore Andre Flo
Tore, Tore Andre Flo

11. Hernan Crespo
(To the tune: *Hello, Hello, I'm Back Again* by Gary Glitter)

Ello, ello, Hernan Crespo, Hernan Crespo

SINGING THE BLUES

The 11 most popular chants at Stamford Bridge

1. One man went to mow
(To the tune: *One Man Went To Mow*)

One man went to mow
Went to mow a meadow
One man and his dog, Spot
Went to mow a meadow
Two men went to mow

etc etc etc (don't forget to leap to your feet when you reach ten)

2. And it's super Chelsea
(To the tune: *The Wild Rover*)

And it's super Chelsea, super Chelsea FC
We're by far the greatest team
The world has ever seen

3. You are my Chelsea
(To the tune: *You Are My Sunshine*)

You are my Chelsea, my only Chelsea
You make me happy when skies are grey
You'll never notice how much I love you
Until you've taken my Chelsea away.
Na, na, na nah nah, Na, na, na nah nah
Whoa-oh-oh-oh-ah, whoa oh-oh-oh…

4. Blue Flag
(To the tune: *Forever and Ever*)
Forever and ever, we'll follow the team
For we are the Chelsea, and we are supreme
We'll never be mastered, by no northern bastards
We'll keep the blue flag flying high.
Flying high up in the sky, we'll keep the blue flag flying high,
From Stamford Bridge to Wembley, we'll keep the blue flag flying high

5. Have you ever seen Chelsea win the league?
(To the tune: *She'll be Coming Round the Mountain*)

Have you ever seen Chelsea win the league?
Have you ever seen Chelsea win the league?
Have you ever seen Chelsea
Ever seen Chelsea
Ever seen Chelsea win the league?
Yes we have!

6. Celery, Celery

Celery, celery
If she don't come
I'll tickle her bum
With a bunch of celery

7. Carefree
(To the tune: *Lord of the Dance*)

Carefree, wherever you may be
We are the famous CFC
And we don't give a f**k
Whoever you may be
'Cos we are the famous CFC

8. We will follow the Chelsea
(To the tune: *Land of Hope and Glory*)

We will follow the Chelsea
Over land and sea (and Leicester)
We will follow the Chelsea
On to victory (altogether now…)

9. Champions League, we're having a laugh
(To the tune: *Tom Hark*)

Champions League, we're having a laugh
Champions League, we're having a laugh
(A song used sneeringly against Chelsea, then appropriated by the Blue choir)

10. Can you hear Arsenal sing?

Can you hear Arsenal sing?
No-o, no-o
Can you hear Arsenal sing?
No-o, no-o
Can you hear Arsenal sing?
I can't hear a f**king thing!
Whoa-oh, oh-oh-oh, oh-oh
Shhhhhhhhhh! Ahhhhhhhh!

(Also directed at any team whose name can be condensed into two syllables)

11. Chel-sea, Chel-sea, Chel-sea, Chel-sea
(To the tune: *Amazing Grace*)

Chel-sea, Chel-sea, Chel-sea, Chel-sea
Chel-sea, Chel-sea, Chel-sea!
(A dirge that has been known to grind on for 30 minutes or more, especially at away games, fading to a gentle buzz before inexplicably rising to a deafening crescendo, whether or not anything of interest is happening on the pitch)

SLAPHEADS

11 shiny Chelsea pates

1. Eddie Newton
2. Gianluca Vialli
3. Frank Sinclair
4. Bryan 'Pop' Robson
5. Michael Duberry
6. Frank Leboeuf
7. William Gallas
8. Ed de Goey
9. Claude Makelele
10. Geremi
11. Juan Sebastian Veron

SMALL TEAM IN FULHAM

11 chants other clubs aim at Chelsea

1. Where were you?

The curiously back-handed compliment used by just about every club. To the tune: *Guide Me, Oh Thou Great Redeemer.*

Where were you, where were you
Where were you when you were shit?

2. Have you ever seen Chelsea win the league?

Used by Manchester United... until 30 April 2005 when it became redundant, and was commandeered, with a twist in the tail, by the Chelsea choir. To the tune: *She'll be coming round the mountain.*

Have you ever seen Chelsea win the league?
Have you ever seen Chelsea win the league?
Have you ever seen Chelsea,
Ever seen Chelsea,
Ever seen Chelsea win the league?
Have you f**k!

3. Where's your money gone?

Tottenham fans' cry as Chelsea conceded a goal at the Bridge in September 2003, weeks after Roman Abramovich's takeover. They'd stopped singing by the end – 4-2 to Chelsea.

Where's your money gone?
Where's your money gone?

"SILVERWARE, NO SILVERWARE, YOU STILL AIN'T GOT NO SILVERWARE"
(FOR HISTORIANS)

4. Shall we win a cup for you?

Arsenal's rapid response to the Chelsea jibe: Shall we buy a ground for you?
To the tune: *Guide Me, Oh Thou Great Redeemer.*

Shall we win
Shall we win
Shall we win a cup for you?

5. The referee's a Russian

Charlton fans' way of communicating their displeasure at a couple of tight offside decisions at Stamford Bridge. To the tune: *The Conga*.

The referee's a Russian
The referee's a Russian

6. Silverware, no silverware

Used by Arsenal and other. To the tune: *The Red Flag*.

Silverware, no silverware
You still ain't got no silverware
From Stamford Bridge to anywhere
You still ain't got no silverware

(NB: of historical interest only)

7. We hate Chelsea

Used by Leeds United. To the tune: *Que Sera Sera*.

When I was just a little boy, I asked my mother what shall I be?
Should I be Chelsea? Should I be Leeds?
Here's what she said to me
Wash your mouth my son, and go get your father's gun
And shoot the Chelsea scum, shoot the Chelsea scum
We hate Chelsea, we hate Chelsea…

8. Champions League

To the tune: *Tom Hark*. Used by just about every club.

Champions League, you're having a laugh…
Champions League, you're having a laugh…

Cunningly adapted and adopted by Chelsea fans. During the Carling Cup game at Reading on 3 December 2003, the Chelsea fans twisted a Reading chant into "Top of the league, we're having a laugh". The same formula has been used for "Premiership, you're having a laugh".

9. Small team in Fulham

Wheeled out by most away fans at some stage. To the tune: *Guantanamera*.

Small team in Fulham
You're just a small team in Fulham…

10. We support our local team
Birmingham City's choir at Stamford Bridge in 2004. To the tune: yet another version of the top church hit *Guide Me, Oh Thou Great Redeemer*.

We support our
We support our
We support our local team!

11. Eng-er-land, Eng-er-land, Eng-er-land…
Used by rival clubs to sneer at Chelsea's imports. To the tune: '*Ere We Go.*

SPARKING UP

11 notorious smokers

1. Eddie McCreadie
As a player and manager, had a 60-a-day ciggy habit.

2. Luca Vialli
Enjoyed cigars.

3. Reg Matthews
Always had a snout in the loo to steady his nerves before a game.

4. Wayne Bridge
Has been spotted having a crafty puff in the players' lounge after a match.

5. Frank Leboeuf
French nicotine addict.

6. John Neal
The manager's office was always filled with clouds of ciggy smoke.

7. Tommy Harmer
'Charmer' Harmer couldn't play without a full-strength pre-match nicotine hit.

8. Mario Stanic
Has always enjoyed a couple of fags while driving home from training.

9. Alan Hudson
Once witnessed running out on to the pitch at the Bridge with a lit cigarette, and chucking the butt on the touchline. Class!

10. Jesper Gronkjær A habitual puffer.

11. Graham Rix A heroic touchline Hamlet smoker.

SQUEEZE UP

11 highest average attendances at the Bridge over one season

1. **48,450** (1954/55)
2. **47,637** (1947/48)
3. **46,943** (1953/54)
4. **46,361** (1948/49)
5. **44,516** (1946/47)
6. **43,842** (1952/53)
7. **42,238** (1949/50)
8. **41,870** (2004/05)
9. **41,855** (2002/03)
10. **41,234** (2003/04)
11. **41,142** (1919/20)

STRANGERS IN BLUE

11 unlikely figures to pull on the blue shirt

1. Jimmy Tarbuck
Came on as a sub for Alan Birchenall in Ken Shellito's testimonial against QPR in 1968.

2. George Best
A bearded Bestie turned up for Peter Osgood's testimonial match in 1975, and played for the Blues.

THE SUPER XI WHO WON THE CUP WINNERS' CUP IN 1971

Peter Bonetti

John Boyle   Ron Harris   John Dempsey   David Webb

Charlie Cooke

Tommy Baldwin

Keith Weller   Peter Houseman

Alan Hudson

Peter Osgood

Even the replay went into extra time at the Karaiskaki stadium, Piraeus, just outside Athens, before Chelsea defeated Real Madrid to lift the club's first piece of European silverware.

3. Matt Busby
There was much switching and swapping during games staged in World War 2, and Sgt Busby – as he was referred to in the programme – pulled on the blue shirt three times for Chelsea, playing at No 4.

4. George Robey
Billed as the Prime Minister of Mirth, the music-hall comedian was on Chelsea's books in the early years. "I have only joined Chelsea so as to keep them in the First Division," he quipped, leading to Chelsea being treated as something of a music-hall joke. "Anyone here from Chelsea Football Club?" was a regular opening gambit by comics surveying the audience. Robey once scored in a friendly.

5. Alan Ball
Played for the Blues in a special match to raise funds for Peter Houseman's orphaned children in March 1977.

6. Walter Winterbottom
The future England manager was a wartime player at Stamford Bridge.

7. Ian Botham
The England cricket captain played in Ron Harris's testimonial in 1980.

8. Joe Mercer
The man who went on to manage England was another of Chelsea's wartime players.

9. Charlie Buchan
The founder of *Charles Buchan's Football Monthly* played for Chelsea during World War 1.

10. Leon Lenik
The Chelsea Restaurant manager swapped his suit for a football kit to run on as sub in Micky Droy's testimonial match in 1983.

11. Dave Beasant
The keeper was the unlikely wearer of a blue shirt during Kerry Dixon's testimonial in 1995, when he came on as a substitute centre-forward… and scored.

SUITS YOU, SIR

11 classic Chelsea kits

1. Royal blue 1971 The fans' favourite. Round-collared, all blue, with gold stars on either side of the club badge to represent the 1970 FA Cup win and the 1971 Cup Winners' Cup victory over Real Madrid. Blue shorts with white stripe down each side, white socks. A true design classic.

2. Blue 1964 Round collar with two narrow white hoops, cuffs ending in three white hoops, and CFC in old-fashioned letters as a breast logo. Blue shorts with white stripe down each side and player number on the front. White socks. As worn by George Graham and Terry Venables.

3. 1950s title-winning kit It's more like a blue rugby shirt with white open-neck collar, white shorts, blue-and-white striped socks.

4. 1979 skintight blue shirt with diamond-shaped Umbro logos down the sleeves and shorts, and a discreet (by today's standards) Umbro logo on the right breast, balanced by the lion badge and two stars. A curious combination of v-neck and open-neck collar. Shorts also had an Umbro motif. White socks.

5. 1974, and as rare as Chelsea away kits come, although repro versions are now sold. One of the most stylish shirts of all time – featuring a bold red vertical stripe next to a bold green vertical stripe on an otherwise white top – but thought to have been worn in earnest on fewer than half a dozen occasions.

6. 1995 blue home kit – the Umbro one, as worn by Ruud Gullit. Open-neck collar with a single button and featuring a bold club badge inside a shield. A return to relative simplicity after years of chopping and changing.

7. 1999 royal blue Autoglass home kit One of the best shirts ever – strong, simple and well-designed, with discreet white piping at the end of the sleeves. Blue shorts with a retro single white stripe on each side.

8. 2003 Emirates home shirt Chelsea's on-field success was mirrored by a meteoric rise in sales of this replica kit. Still less frippery. Simple white collar.

9. 1998 white away kit Initially it made fans think of the hated Leeds United or Spurs, but there was no denying it looked good on the lads. Royal blue piping on collar and cuffs helped.

10. 2002 midnight blue One of the finest away kits in Premiership history and the best Emirates shirt of the lot.

11. 1981 mustard yellow with thin vertical stripes and centrally-sited club badge. Subtle red piping on a simple v-neck collar. Oddly attractive.

THESE LADS ARE A BIT MIXED UP

A team of Chelsea anagrams

1. **Perch etc** Petr Cech
2. **I run acid colic** Carlo Cudicini
3. **Or a life up the rear** Paulo Ferreira
4. **Winey badger** Wayne Bridge
5. **U R the throb** Robert Huth
6. **Early men sex it** Alexey Smertin
7. **Elude camel leak** Claude Makelele
8. **Dead muffin** Damien Duff
9. **Top trackers** Scott Parker
10. **Odd brigadier** Didier Drogba
11. **He is judged on run** Eidur Gudjohnsen

Manager: Sure, John, I moo (José Mourinho)
Owner: Rob a rich ammo van (Roman Abramovich)

THESE LADS DID WELL

Chelsea's top-scorers in a single season

1. **Jimmy Greaves** 43 goals (1960/61)
2. **Jimmy Greaves** 37 goals (1958/59)
   Bobby Tambling 37 goals (1962/63)
4. **Kerry Dixon** 36 goals (1984/85)
5. **Kerry Dixon** 34 goals (1983/84)
   Bob Whittingham 34 goals (1910/11)
7. **Peter Osgood** 31 goals (1969/70)

Peter Osgood 31 goals (1971/72)
9. **Hughie Gallacher** 30 goals (1931/32)
   Jimmy Greaves 30 goals (1959/60)
   George Hilsdon 30 goals (1907/08)
   Tommy Lawton 30 goals (1946/47)
   Bob Turnbull 30 goals (1925/26)

TOP BRASS

11 fascinating facts from the Chelsea boardroom

1. Ken Bates became a director at Chelsea in 1981, and was the club's third longest-serving chairman.

2. Matthew Harding the club director died in a helicopter crash while returning from an away match on 22 October 1996.

3. The largest number of directors at the club was **seven**, between 1905 and 1907.

4. The longest serving director was **Claude Kirby**, who chaired the board throughout his 30 years at the club from 1905 to 1935.

5. Dickie Attenborough, a director from 1969-82, is now life vice-president.

6. Vivian Woodward, who played for Chelsea from 1909-15, is the only former player to become a director. He was on the board from 1922-30.

7. Yvonne Todd was the first female board member, joining in the Ken Bates era.

8. John Neal is the only Chelsea manager to have served on the board, from 1985-6.

9. Viscount Chelsea, the late Lord Cadogan, was a director from 1964-83, and chairman for two years.

10. Between 1905, when the club was set up, and 1983, there was always a member of the **Mears family** on the board.

11. A father and son, both called **C.J. Pratt**, were board members at Chelsea. Dad was chairman in 1936, junior from 1966-68.

TOUGH NUTS

Not so much born as quarried – 11 Chelsea hard men

1. Ken Armstrong 1946-57
Ferocious tackler who joined the Blues after World War 2 and was a key part of the defensive foundation on which the 1955 title-winning season was built. His will specified that his ashes should be scattered on the Stamford Bridge turf, so he was still able to get under opponents' feet.

2. Ron Harris 1963-80
He'd have your legs away soon as look at you. Chopper took no prisoners and never, ever, pulled out of a tackle. For 17 years he was a rock for Chelsea, and was one of the few defenders in the land to be able to nullify the threat of Jimmy Greaves when the striker was playing for Spurs.

3. Micky Droy 1970-85
A courageous and strong tackler, he would hurl his 6ft 4in, 15-stone frame at visiting forwards. So scary he was often pushed forward to frighten opposing defenders.

4. Dennis Rofe 1980-82
Full-back who found it far more effective to intercept the man than the ball. Hailed as the heaven-sent replacement for Chopper Harris.

5. Joey Jones 1982-85
Picked on by press and rival fans for his wholehearted tackles and manic disregard for the pain inflicted on opponents. His reputation followed the Welshman down from Liverpool and was further enhanced at Stamford Bridge.

> SPEEDIE FOUGHT FOR CHELSEA UNTIL THE FINAL WHISTLE... THEN CARRIED ON IN THE TUNNEL

6. David Speedie 1982-87
Put it this way, you wouldn't argue if he got pushy in a pub. The fiery Scot with a notoriously short fuse fired 64 goals in 197 appearances and fought for Chelsea until the final whistle… then carried on in the tunnel.

7. Doug Rougvie 1984-87
A solid wall it was inadvisable to run into, he could put a man in hospital with one scythe of his leg – before punting the ball out of the ground. A commentator once said of the no-nonsense bludgeoner (signed from Aberdeen) that if he was used as a scarecrow, the crows would bring the corn back. Oddly enough, Doug was a very

mild character off the pitch and his wife was very much the dominant force in their marriage, deciding which clubs he would sign for after leaving the Bridge.

8. Graham Roberts 1988-90
Battle-hardened with huge thighs and an expression which told opponents "Just you dare!" A born leader, he traded on his hard-man image to intimidate and inspire.

9. Dennis Wise 1990-2001
At first sight more of a terrier than a hard man, but the impish ex-member of Wimbledon's Crazy Gang had a fierce temper which left visitors nursing injuries and the little man contemplating the game from the stands during spells of suspension.

10. Vinnie Jones 1991-92
Tattooed, thuggish destroyer. Jones had no regard for anyone, and muscled every fancy dan off the ball, to the glee of the terrace faithful. A gloriously violent player, he was feared by most opponents. Now perfectly cast as a big-screen hard man.

11. Mark Hughes 1995-98
For such a quietly spoken, mild-mannered family man off the pitch, the striker with the salt-and-pepper hair was a mad axeman on it. "I was able to get rid of any frustrations I had on the football field," Sparky once remarked. Many contemporaries can still point to scars on their legs and say "Hughes".

TRADESMEN'S ENTRANCE
The jobs of 11 Blues before they joined Chelsea

1. **Kenny Swain** schoolteacher
2. **Eddie McCreadie** shop window dresser
3. **Eric Parsons** poster designer
4. **Johnny Jackson** draughtsman
5. **Vinnie Jones** hod carrier
6. **Ralph Oelefse** civil engineer
7. **Kevin Hitchcock** electrician
8. **Johnny McNichol** mechanic
9. **Jimmy Greaves** telephone exchange operator
10. **Tommy Lawton** golf club maker
11. **Kerry Dixon** toolmaker

TRANSFER LANDMARKS

11 Chelsea records in player acquisitions

1. **Fred Rouse** (1907) at £1,000, Chelsea's first four-figure buy
2. **Hughie Gallagher** (1930) Chelsea's first £10,000 player
3. **Reg Matthews** (1956) £20,000 was the world record for a keeper
4. **Tony Hateley** (1966) Chelsea's first £100,000 player
5. **Dave Beasant** (1989) Chelsea's first £500,000 signing
6. **Dennis Wise** (1990) The club's first £1m player
7. **Frode Grodas** (1996) Chelsea's first free signing under the Bosman ruling
8. **Roberto Di Matteo** (1996) £4.9m was a new Chelsea record
9. **Graeme Le Saux** (1997) Became the first player to break the £5m barrier
10. **Ricardo Carvalho** (2004) £19.85m of Roman's dosh was handed to Porto
11. **Didier Drogba** (2004) £24m splashed out on another striker

TRIPLE-BARRELLED

11 Chelsea players with three names

1. Peter Rhoades-Brown
2. Jimmy Floyd Hasselbaink
3. Ian Tait Robertson
4. Roberto Di Matteo
5. Ed de Goey
6. Ben Howard Baker
7. Graeme Le Saux
8. Tore Andre Flo
9. Sam dalla Bona
10. Enrique de Lucas
11. Juan Sebastian Veron

TRUE BLUES

The 11 players who've made the most appearances for Chelsea

1. **Ron Harris** (1961-79) 795
2. **Peter Bonetti** (1959-78 729
3. **John Hollins** (1963-83) 592

4. **Dennis Wise** (1990-2001) 445
5. **Steve Clarke** (1987-98) 421
6. **Kerry Dixon** (1983-92) 420
7. **Eddie McCreadie** (1962-73) 410
8. **Ken Armstrong** (1947-56) 402
9. **Peter Osgood** (1964-79) 380
10. **Charlie Cooke** (1965-77) 373
11. **George Smith** (1921-31) 370
    Bobby Tambling (1958-69) 370

TUMBLING RECORDS

Milestones and achievements from the extraordinary 2004/5 season

1. All-time top-flight points record
The 95 points from 38 games easily beats Man Utd's 92 points from 42 games, set in 1993/94. Chelsea's previous best was 79 in 2003/04. The club's best in any division remains 99 in the old Division 2 in 1988/99 (over 46 games).

2. Fewest league goals conceded
Chelsea leaked a miserly 15, beating Liverpool's 1978/79 record by one (though, to be fair, the Scousers played four more games in the season). Until 2004/05 Arsenal had the best Premiership stats with 17 conceded in 1998/09. Chelsea's previous best was 30 in 1998/99 and 2003/04.

3. The most Premiership clean sheets
The 1-0 victory over Charlton in May 2005 took the tally to 25, pipping Man Utd's 24 in 1994/95 (achieved over 42 games, not 38). The Blues' previous best was 21 in 2003/04. Chelsea's 34 clean sheets in all competitions set a new club record. Only Liverpool have ever done better in the top flight, with 28 clean sheets over 42 games in 1978/79.

4. Premiership clean sheet record
Petr Cech's 1,024 Premiership minutes without conceding a goal eclipsed Peter Schmiechel's 1997 total of 694.

5. Most Chelsea league wins in a season
Victory at Old Trafford in May 2005 equalled the club's all-time record of 29 league wins (in Division 2, 1988/89, set over 46 games) and beat Chelsea's top-flight record of 24 set in 1964/65 and repeated in 2003/04.

6. Fewest league defeats
Just the one, against Man City on 16 October 2004. Best previous total was three in 1998/99. Only Arsenal have gone a whole season undefeated.

7. Most league doubles
A dozen beats the previous best of eight in 1906/07 and 1962/63 (both Division 2).

8. Most consecutive clean sheets in top-flight football
Ten beats Liverpool's previous record of eight, set in 1922/23, equalled by Arsenal in 1998/99.

9. Most consecutive away wins in the top-flight
Nine was one more than Chelsea's previous best achievement – eight on the spin in 1988/89 in Division 2.

10. Best goal difference
Chelsea's previous total of 53 had stood since the club's first season, 1905/06. A century later, 57 was the tally.

11. Most consecutive appearances for an outfield player
Frank Lampard's 146 consecutive Premiership games at the end of 2004/05 set a new record for an outfield player. Goalie David James still held the record for all players of 159. Chelsea's previous club best was John Hollins (135).

TWITCHERS' CORNER

11 ornithological connections

1. John Sparrow
2. Jack Cock
3. Gavin Peacock
4. Ted Drake
5. Tommy Boyd (geddit?)
6. William Dickie
7. Samuel Weaver
8. Arjen Robben
9. Alfred Bower
10. A Bird (no first name recorded, but he made eight wartime appearances in the 1918/19 season, and was fifth highest scorer with four goals)
11. Winston Bogarde (nicknamed De Ekster in his native Holland. It means "the magpie" – apparently because of all the necklaces and rings he acquired)

"WE NEEDED THE MONEY"

11 other activities which have taken place in or around Stamford Bridge

1. Athletics
2. Greyhound racing
3. Speedway
4. Rugby league
5. Rugby union
6. Cricket
7. Baseball
8. Midget car racing
9. American football
10. Highland games
11. Weddings

"WE'RE GONNA WIN THE GLASGOW MERCHANTS CUP!"

11 glorious triumphs that are curiously overlooked today

1. **London Victory Cup** 1919
2. **Football League (South) Cup** 1945
3. **The Festival of Britain Trophy** 1951
4. **Southern Junior Floodlit Cup** 1959
5. **The Glasgow Merchants Cup** 1965
6. **The Prince Philip Cup** 1975
7. **Full Members' Cup** 1986
8. **Zenith Data Systems Cup** 1990
9. **Cross-Channel Cup** 1993

10. The Makita Trophy 1993
11. The Umbro Cup 1996

WHAT ARE THE CHANCES OF THAT?

11 bizarre Chelsea goals

1. Alan Hudson was awarded the craziest goal at Stamford Bridge. It was against Ipswich, September 1970. Huddy thumped the ball goalwards from 20 yards out, and it missed… but billowed the side-netting. The ref mistakenly thought it had gone in, turned away and pointed to the centre spot. The Ipswich players besieged referee and linesman, but to no avail. The goal stood, and Chelsea won 2-1. "Phantom winner" screamed one headline the next day.

2. Gianluca Vialli scored when the ball ricocheted off his bottom and into the net in a blizzard at Tromso in the Cup Winners' Cup second round game in October 1997.

3. Ben Whitehouse's goal against Blackburn Rovers on 2 December 1907. Had you been 13 seconds late getting to Stamford Bridge, you'd have missed it. A century on, it's still the club's fastest league strike. Neither goalie was troubled for the following 89 minutes 47 seconds; it stayed 1-0.

4. Paul Canoville came on as sub at the beginning of the second half of Chelsea's League Cup quarter-final replay against Sheffield Wednesday at Hillsborough in January 1985, and scored after 11 seconds.

5. Selhurst Park, November 1971. **Alan Hudson** took a corner… and it missed everybody and swung straight into the goal. "I got the idea from watching Johann Cruyff in pre-season, curling in crosses," he said afterwards. Yeah, sure. It finished Crystal Palace 2, Chelsea 3.

6. Chelsea's second in the 3-1 win over Leicester City at Stamford Bridge in December 1954 is a true collectors' item and a pub quizzer's dream: **a shared own-goal** – the only one in English league history. Johnny McNichol's shot hit the bar and bounced down. Leicester's Stan Milburn and Jack Froggatt swung at it simultaneously, but only succeeded in wellying it into the back of their own net. "It was quite impossible to divide it, so they had to shoulder the responsibility together, each angrily blaming the other," said McNichol, choking back tears of laughter afterwards.

7. On 18 May 1963, Chelsea were pushing for promotion, and needed a win against Sunderland. They nicked the points thanks to a curious goal by midfielder **Tommy Harmer**. Bobby Tambling's corner kick flew into the Sunderland goalmouth, struck Harmer amidships and rebounded into the net. Cockney rhyming slang aficionados will appreciate the line used ever since, that Harmer scored with his "hickory".

8. Dennis Wise scored many important goals for Chelsea, but his only goal for England – on his debut against Turkey in a European Nations Cup qualifier – remains the subject of heated debate. It either went in off his bottom or his arm.

9. It may be the custom to wait for one or two colleagues to get forward before taking a free kick, but **Alan Hudson** was never one for convention. On 5 January 1972 at White Hart Lane (in the second leg of a League Cup semi-final), Mike England gave away a foul by the corner flag. John Hollins might have been expected to trot forward to take it, but Hudson fired in a quick low drive. With no Chelsea players anywhere near the area, keeper Pat Jennings left it to Cyril Knowles to boot away, but Knowles flailed at the ball, which hit the far post and, as 52,755 people watched in amazement, dribbled over the line to knock Spurs out in the dying moments. Nice one, Cyril.

10. Frank Sinclair's goal which helped defeat Middlesbrough in the 1998 League Cup final led to fair bit of ribbing for the defender. Dennis Wise flew down the right and crossed. Sinclair tripped and fell forward, the ball hit his head and flew in.

11. Joe Allon scored on his debut in 1991, but didn't know a great deal about it. It was another "hickory" goal, the ball striking him in the groin and rebounding into the goal.

WHAT DO I HAVE TO DO TO MAKE YOU LOVE ME?

11 Chelsea greats never fully appreciated by England managers

1. **Alan Hudson** 2 caps
2. **Terry Venables** 2 caps
3. **Bobby Tambling** 3 caps
4. **Peter Brabrook** 3 caps
5. **George Mills** 3 caps
6. **Keith Weller** 4 caps
7. **Peter Osgood** 4 caps
8. **Barry Bridges** 4 caps
9. **Kerry Dixon** 5 caps

10. Frank Blunstone 5 caps
11. Peter Bonetti 7 caps

WHAT'S IN A NAME?

The 11 most common first names for Chelsea players before World War 2

1. **James** 23
2. **William** 20
3. **George** 18
   Robert 18
5. **John** 12
6. **Thomas** 9
7. **Joseph** 7
8. **Harold** 6
   Jack 6
   Frank 6
11. **David** 5
   Edward 5
   Sidney 5
   Sam 5
   Arthur 5

WHERE WERE YOU WHEN WE WEREN'T SO GOOD?

The 11 lowest average home attendances in any single season at the Bridge

1. **12,737** 1982/83
2. **13,132** 1981/82
3. **14,368** 1905/06
4. **15,957** 1988/89
5. **17,578** 1906/07
6. **17,694** 1986/87
7. **17,896** 1980/81
8. **18,754** 1992/93
9. **18,779** 1991/92
10. **18,956** 1975/76
11. **19,244** 1993/94

WHO ARE YA?
11 alternative names for Chelsea FC

1. London FC
When the Stamford Bridge stadium was built on the site of the old London Athletic Club track, it was decided to form a new club. London FC was a leading suggestion.

2. Kensington FC
An alternative name proposed for the club ahead of the first season.

3. The Chinaman
Suggested as the club nickname by readers of the *Fulham Chronicle* when Chelsea was inaugurated – because of Chelsea pottery.

4. The Buns
Another rejected effort from readers in the competition to find a suitable moniker.

5. The Pensioners
The original tag from the early 20th century, because of the famous red-jacketed Chelsea Pensioners at the Royal Hospital.

6. Tudor Rose
The quirky codename for Chelsea's youth scheme, launched in 1947 by Billy Birrell.

7. Drake's Ducklings
The press nickname for Ted Drake's young homegrown talent of the early 1950s – the team that went on to win the title in 1955.

8. The Blues
Manager Drake's 'modern' nickname for the club, chosen because he felt that "Pensioners" was conveying an altogether too decrepit image.

9. Docherty's Diamonds
Tommy Docherty's stars were dubbed the Diamonds. It was apt.

10. Chelski
The name immediately bestowed on the boys from SW6 in the aftermath of Roman Abramovich's Russian revolution. It may have stuck among the envious but it's wrong. The suffix '-ski' would make them Polish. It would have to be '-kov' to be Russian, but 'Chelskov' doesn't have quite the same ring.

11. Mourinho's Marvels
First spotted in newspapers in 2004 to describe the superteam of 2004/05.

THE WONDER THAT IS THE WORLDWIDE WEB

The Blues in cyberspace

1. Official club site (www.chelseafc.com) The official Chelsea club site, with years of news, exhaustive match reports, player information and history sections (although the spellings of some past stars names are so inaccurate it's a lottery looking them up). The inevitable links to ticket sales, megastore merchandise and betting sites.

2. Chelsea Desktop Wallpaper (www.chelsea-desktop-wallpaper.co.uk) Click on 'Seasons Past' for a comprehensive season-by-season guide to league results, player appearances and stats – mostly accurate, but with one or two oddities. Tottenham are referred to as Tottenham Hotspurs, suggesting that someone with no knowledge of the game did the keying in. One or two entertaining reminiscence pieces about the good old Shed.

3. CFC Net (www.cfc-net.co.uk) Billed as 'the intelligent forum' for fans of the champions, the site has its roots in the Chelsea Independent Supporters' Association (which had many spirited disagreements and run-ins with Ken Bates). Readable, opinionated match reports and a busy, popular fans' forum.

4. Chelsea FC Supporters Registry (www.chelsea-fc.com) The site of the Chelsea Supporters Registry brags it's the oldest Chelsea site on the web. A lively forum, strong opinions, plenty of links, polls and stats.

5. Chelsea Mad (www.chelsea-mad.co.uk) News, views, messageboards, archives.

6. CFC Songs (www.nicholas.harrison.mcmail.com/cfcsong4.htm) Huge resource of uncensored Chelsea chants down the years, many with historical context.

7. Chelsea Old Boys FC (www.chelseaoldboys.co.uk) Chummy little site proving that there is life after Chelsea for former players who get together for charity matches, and plug their availability for after-dinner speaking.

8. Chelsea FC (www.mychelseafc.com) Tables, results, news, data and a chance to vote for players of the match.

9. Chelsea FC Blog (www.chelseablog.com) Well-connected site with links to just about everything to do with the club. A good starting point.

10. Fans FC (www.fansfc.com/chelsea) Forum, news and links to other clubs' sites.

11. 4 The Game (www.4thegame.com/club/cfc) A blizzard of news, stats, player profiles and links.

WONDERFUL GOALS GALORE

11 superlative strikes by Chelsea players

1. Robbie Di Matteo 17 May 1997, Chelsea 2 Middlesbrough 0
Half a minute into the FA Cup final, Di Matteo collected a short pass from Dennis Wise in his own half, surged forward and unleashed the sweetest long-range strike imaginable. It soared over keeper Ben Roberts, dipped, grazed the underside of the bar and billowed the net. There were precisely 43 seconds on the clock.

2. John Hollins 29 August 1970, Chelsea 2 Arsenal 1
Hollins chipped Bob Wilson in the Arsenal goal but the ball came back off the bar. Hollins corkscrewed round and hooked the rebound over his shoulder, over the helpless Wilson and into the net, comfortably winning ITV's Goal of the Season.

3. Gianfranco Zola 16 January 2002, Chelsea 4 Norwich City 0
The third of Chelsea's goals that demolished Norwich in this FA Cup third round replay was sheer Zola wizardry. He ran forward to meet Graeme Le Saux's 62nd-minute corner, and back-flicked the ball in mid-air through his own legs and into the net. No superlative is adequate. Later he brought tears to the eyes of hard-bitten hacks by dedicating the wondergoal to an eight-year-old he had visited in hospital days before, revealing that the little lad had since died of cancer.

4. John Spencer 3 November 1994, Austria Memphis 1 Chelsea 1
Ran the length of the pitch to score in the Cup Winners' Cup. He received the ball from a cleared corner by the Blues' opponents, then set off towards goal from well inside his own half, his little legs pumping up and down like pistons. It almost seemed as if the wee fellow was alone on the pitch. Nobody could catch him, and he beat the keeper. It was the vital away goal that meant Chelsea progressed to meet Bruges in the next round.

5. Bjarne Goldbaek 10 May 1999, Tottenham Hotspur 2 Chelsea 2
Danced down the right flank at Three Point Lane and fired a rocket from 35 yards to deny Spurs victory for the umpteenth time. It almost broke the net and left players, fans and teammates on the bench open-mouthed in amazement. Computer technology later measured the shot, speed at 66.1 mph – 36 mph more than the speed limit in the road outside.

6. Clive Walker 7 May 1983, Bolton Wanderers 0 Chelsea 1
Freed down the left by a Paul Canoville pass in the penultimate game of the season, Walker sent a 25-yard shot curling into the top corner of the net. It was arguably the most important goal any player had ever scored for Chelsea because it meant the Blues avoided potentially catastrophic relegation to Division 3.

7. Peter Osgood 17 March 1973, score Chelsea 2 Arsenal 2
Osgood's 20-yard left-foot volley in this FA Cup quarter final is one of the most repeated television goals of all time, and deservedly won the BBC Goal of the Season competition.

8. Eddie McCreadie 15 March 1965, Chelsea 3 Leicester City 2
On as an emergency centre-forward in the first (home) leg of the League Cup final, the full-back took the ball from the halfway line, beat five opponents, rounded Gordon Banks and rifled home. It was a vital strike too – Chelsea won 3-2 and drew the return leg 0-0 to lift the trophy.

9. Bob Whittingham 20 March 1912, Gainsborough Trinity 0 Chelsea 2
Whittingham, who scored 80 goals in 129 appearances, hit the ball so hard that it knocked the Trinity goalkeeper clean off his feet and powered on across the line.

10. Eidur Gudjohnsen 28 January 2003, Chelsea 3 Leeds United 2
Frank Lampard drifted right and floated over a perfect cross. The Icelander met it with an exquisite bicycle kick that sent the ball rocketing past a helpless Paul Robinson.

11. Kerry Dixon 25 August 1984, Arsenal 1 Chelsea 1
On the opening day of the 1984/5 season, Doug Rougvie took a free kick on the left. Kerry Dixon trapped the ball, turned and slammed it, left-footed, at the Arsenal goal. Pat Jennings saved, but the ball came out again to Dixon, who switched effortlessly to his right foot and sent an unstoppable volley into the net.

WORST LEAGUE SEQUENCE

The 11 results at the end of Chelsea's 1961/62 season

1. Chelsea 1 Birmingham City 1
2. Everton 4 Chelsea 0
3. Chelsea 2 Arsenal 3
4. Bolton Wanderers 4 Chelsea 2
5. Chelsea 1 Manchester City 1
6. Leicester City 2 Chelsea 0
7. West Bromwich Albion 4 Chelsea 0
8. Chelsea 4 Wolves 5
9. Chelsea 2 Ipswich Town 2
10. Wolves 1 Chelsea 1
11. Burnley 1 Chelsea 1

Tommy Docherty took over from Ted Drake in October 1961, but it wasn't enough to halt Chelsea's miserable slide into the old Division 2. Eleven games without a win is the Blues' worst sequence. The team, characterised by the press as lazy playboys, finished with 28 points and were dumped out of the FA Cup by Liverpool.

WOT? NO PIES?

11 favourite pre-match meals

1. **Gianluca Vialli** well-done roast chicken and rice
2. **Graeme Le Saux** roast chicken with spaghetti
3. **Gianfranco Zola** pasta, parmesan cheese, rice
4. **Frank Leboeuf** fish, pasta and rice
5. **Celestina Babayaro** cheese omelette and baked beans
6. **Mark Hughes** roast chicken breast and pasta
7. **Roberto Di Matteo** cereal
8. **Frank Sinclair** ham omelette
9. **Tore Andre Flo** spaghetti with bolognese sauce
10. **Mark Nicholls** baked beans on toast
11. **Willie Foulke** all the above. The Blues' first goalie once famously arrived in a hotel dining room before the rest of the team and polished off all 11 platefuls of food that had been set out.

GOALIE FOULKE HAD A FEROCIOUS APPETITE, ONCE POLISHING OFF 11 PLATEFULS OF FOOD BEFORE A MATCH

X-FILES

Totally random trivia that couldn't find a home anywhere else

1. Menial jobs Jimmy Greaves lived in a flat in the main stand at Plough Lane, and had to weed the terraces as part of the tenancy agreement.

2. Hair-raising sidelines Dave Webb once part-owned a wig shop.

3. Embarrassing defeats The Blues were the laughing stock of Europe three seasons running after being dumped out of the UEFA Cup at early stages by such exalted names as St Gallen (2000), Hapoel Tel Aviv (2001) and Viking FK (2002).

4. Flimsy excuses Back-pedalling from his UEFA stand-off, José Mourinho blamed inflammatory words on his poor English. Oh yeah? The man could teach the subject!

5. Terrace fashions Turn-ups... until fag-ends fell in them and kept smouldering.

6. Bogey team Chelsea are unwelcome visitors at Old Trafford (they've lost just four times in 30 visits) and White Hart Lane (unbeaten in the league since 1987).

7. Buddies David Copeland and John Kirwan won the FA Cup with Spurs in 1901, then felt they couldn't face separation, and moved together to Chelsea in 1905. Ahh.

8. Hue what? Chelsea's royal blue is ex-president Lord Cadogan's racing colour.

9. How much? Juan Sebastian Veron's 14 run-outs cost Chelsea £1,071,428 apiece.

10. Quackers Roman Abramovich once sold plastic ducks from his Moscow flat.

11. Inflation Barrage balloons saved the Bridge from bombers in wartime games.

YOUR USUAL, SIR?

11 eateries with a Chelsea flavour

1. La Familigia In Langton Street, Chelsea. Run by Alvaro Maccioni. Booking essential. Carlo Cudicini is a regular and Roman Abramovich has been spotted there.

2. Blue Spice Fulham Road. Once known as the East India, this is the favoured curry haunt of fans, 100 yards from the ground. Matchday demand – before and after games – is so great that the tables extend into a room at the back.

3. Blue Elephant Fulham Road. Near the old entrance to Fulham Broadway tube station, it's where the posh people eat. Upmarket and pricey Thai food in an exotic setting with a small stream running through the restaurant.

4. Barbarella's Fulham Road. Almost enveloped by Stamford Bridge – look for the discreet canopied entrance. Features such dishes as noodles with baby lobster (£13). A favourite haunt of Chelsea players in the 1960s, its ambience was described by Alan Hudson as "like that lovely atmosphere you see in gangster movies like *The Godfather* and *Goodfellas*".

5. Café Brazil Fulham Road. The place for street barbecues before home games. Also serves pizzas and jumbo hot dogs.

6. Conrad Hotel Chelsea Harbour. Best to wear a tie and take a credit card with a very big limit. It's popular with Chelsea players. Roman's eaten there and Claudio Ranieri loved the Sunday brunches.

7. Julie's Too Café At the junction of Moore Park Road and Fulham Road, near the main entrance to the Bridge. Sarnies and cuppas before a game.

8. Fishnets In the Chelsea Village complex. Matchday menu is £25 for two courses, but the same kitchens churn out perfectly good fish and chips for a fiver if you don't mind joining the long queue snaking towards the side window.

9. La Reserve Hotel Fulham Road. Things have improved on the burger front since the 1970s caravans that served brown cardboard between slices of white cardboard. It's now £3 for burgers, cheeseburgers or jumbo hot dogs from the trailer in the La Reserve forecourt or the one tethered inside the main entrance to the ground.

10. Arkles In the middle of Chelsea Village, yards from the pitch. This is the place for a Gaelic knees-up, to be sure, but it's very much upmarket Irish fare. Just the place if you fancy a piece of salmon on a fennel and tomato compote.

11. The Lost Café Now well and truly lost. It vanished in the Fulham Broadway redevelopment, but many fans have happy memories of the curious subterranean café which once specialised in filled baked potatoes, all-day breakfasts, cake and sandwiches and – bizarrely – featured pictures of the Copacabana beach on the walls.

YOU'RE STANDING ON MY FOOT

The 11 largest attendances at Stamford Bridge

1. 100,000 Chelsea v Moscow Dynamo, 13 November 1945
With 74,496 officially inside, the fences collapsed because of the sheer weight of numbers remaining outside. Estimates vary, but 100,000 spectators (many on the roof of the stands) is the consensus.

2. 82,905 Chelsea v Arsenal, 12 October 1935.

3. 77,952 Chelsea v Swindon Town (FA Cup fourth round), 13 March 1911.

4. 77,696 Chelsea v Blackpool, 16 October 1948.

5. 76,000 Chelsea v Tottenham Hotspur, 16 October 1920 (estimated figure).

6. 75,952 Chelsea v Arsenal, 9 October 1937.

7. 75,334 Chelsea v Arsenal, 29 November 1930.

8. 75,043 Chelsea v Wolverhampton Wanderers, 9 April 1955.

9. 75,000 England v Switzerland, 11 May 1946 (estimated figure).

10. 74,365 Chelsea v Birmingham City (FA Cup sixth round replay), 4 March 1931.

11. 74,190 Chelsea v Arsenal, 22 April 1933.

THE SHEER WEIGHT OF 100,000 FANS BROKE DOWN THE FENCES AT STAMFORD BRIDGE IN 1945

"The Luther Blissetts don't exist. Only Luther Blissett exists"

Italian anarchists, who used the AC Milan striker's identity in court, 'clarify' matters

If this Rough Guide has struck a chord, do yourself a favour and seek out the Rough Guide to Cult Football, probably the oddest football book ever written, covering iconic stars, pointless clubs, the cups that time forgot and Pelé's secret career as a guitar axe man. Failing that, you may enjoy the Rough Guides to Superheroes, Cult Movies, Cult Fiction and Muhammad Ali. Essential, compact reading, these books are almost as good as having three points in the bag.